WORDS
OF THE WORD

GOD'S WORD IS OUR GREAT HERITAGE
LUTHERAN SERVICE BOOK 582

Ron Stieglitz

ISBN 978-1-63903-930-2 (paperback)
ISBN 978-1-63903-931-9 (digital)

Christian Faith Publishing, Inc.
832 Park Avenue
Meadville, PA 16335
www.christianfaithpublishing.com

Printed in the United States of America

To Bev, my wife,
You have everything to do with everything I do.
All my love, always!

Contents

Acknowledgments

A number of people have read all or parts of the several iterations of the text and have offered suggestions and/or encouragement: my wife, Bev, my late friend Wally Bohler, Chris Nelson, Rev. Nathan Lewis, Rev. Timothy Shoup, and Dr. Rev. Dwayne Luecke. I thank them and appreciate their comments. However, any errors are solely mine.

Introduction

We live and breathe words.

—Cassandra Clare

We would agree that words are important to us—some more than others but nevertheless important. The kind words of a friend or spouse are a treasure that supports us in a time of trouble, whereas a politician's words of promise might be received with skepticism or even scorn. We use words to communicate and share information with each other. We employ words to express happiness, approval, and satisfaction, as well as sadness, anger, and frustration. In spite of the old saying that was often used to respond to an insult or put-down, "Sticks and stones may break my bones, but words will never hurt me," words can wound us deeply. Words can also be uplifting. If someone remarks to us, "Great work on that contract," "Fantastic play in the game," or "You look so good in that outfit," our day is improved.

On the other hand, words can be confusing if not meaningless to us. That is the case when they are unfamiliar or infrequently encountered. For instance, how many of us use the term *dialectics,* meaning the science of reasoning or debate, in everyday conversation? I chose that word because I had encountered it in the past but still had to find its exact meaning in a dictionary to refresh my memory. Foreign words used in a sentence by an author for effect or as the language of an entire document also can be unintelligible to most of us. Who has not unpacked our latest electronic purchase, unfolded the instructions, and stared at a page with a language not only with words we do not recognize but also composed of characters that are unlike anything we are used to (Figure 1)? Fortunately, we can turn the pages to find the section written in our native language to continue the struggle to assemble the tool or set up the device.

注意：如果您使用繁體中文，您可以免費獲得語言援助服務。請致電 1-877-533-5020 (TTY: 1-800-947-3529)

ACHTUNG: Wenn Sie Deutsch sprechen, stehen Ihnen kostenlos sprachliche Hilfsdienstleistungen zur Verfügung. Rufnummer: 1-877-533-5020 (TTY: 1-800-947-3529).

ملحوظة: إذا كنت تتحدث اذكر اللغة، فإن خدمات المساعدة اللغوية تتوافر لك بالمجان. اتصل برقم 1-5020-533-877 (رقم هاتف الصم والبكم: 1-3529-947-800).

ВНИМАНИЕ: Если вы говорите на русском языке, то вам доступны бесплатные услуги перевода. Звоните 1-877-533-5020 (телетайп: 1-800-947-3529).

주의: 한국어를 사용하시는 경우, 언어 지원 서비스를 무료로 이용하실 수 있습니다. 1-877-533-5020 (TTY: 1-800-947-3529)번으로 전화해 주십시오.

CHÚ Ý: Nếu bạn nói Tiếng Việt, có các dịch vụ hỗ trợ ngôn ngữ miễn phí dành cho bạn. Gọi số 1-877-533-5020 (TTY: 1-800-947-3529).

Wann du [Deitsch (Pennsylvania German / Dutch)] schwetzscht, kannscht du mitaus Koschte ebber gricke, ass dihr helft mit die englisch Schprooch. Ruf selli Nummer uff: Call 1-877-533-5020 (TTY: 1-800-947-3529).

ໂປດຊາບ: ຖ້າ ວ່າ ທ່ານ ເວົ້າ ພາສາ ລາວ, ການ ບໍລິການ ຊ່ວຍເຫຼືອ ດ້ານ ພາສາ, ໂດຍບໍ່ ເສັຽຄ່າ, ແມ່ນ ມີ ພ້ອມ ໃຫ້ ທ່ານ. ໂທຣ 1-877-533-5020 (TTY: 1-800-947-3529).

Figure 1. Foreign Language Customer Service Contacts

At other times, the problem lies with us. Our comprehension or retention of the definition of a word or concept is sketchy. We feel that we understand a word, but we are unsure and struggle to express it clearly. When I began to read the Bible more thoughtfully and paid better attention in worship services, I was stunned by the number of words and terms that I stumbled over, did not thoroughly understand, or whose deeper meaning had little appreciation of. Of course, I had always come across words in passages that were difficult to pronounce and less than familiar. Even a seemingly common word might defy my attempt to grasps its definition, relevance, or significance in context. I was somewhat relieved when I realized through conversations with family, friends, and fellow church members that I was not alone. This problem was not only my problem.

There is a long list of words associated with the Christian religion. Some have precise definitions, whereas others convey entire rich concepts or ideas and some can be confusing, if not intimidating. It is not my purpose to produce another alphabetical Bible dictionary or a dictionary of the Christian Religion. There are good available ones of each. Nor will this be an in-depth and comprehensive study of the beliefs and teachings, that is, the *doctrines*, of the Christian Church. I am not qualified to do that. Rather, my goal is to assist not only new Christians, but also long-time adherents in the pew on Sunday morning, in a Bible class, or engaged in personal study to better understand and appreciate the words that they hear or read. I would like this to be a refresher for veteran Christians looking to develop a deeper understanding of their faith and a primer for new Christians who are trying to build a foundation for theirs. I did not cite or quote multiple Bible passages for each word or concept that provide nuances of meaning from somewhat different perspectives. That approach is for detailed studies. Instead, I have selected passages that seem to adequately introduce and clearly explain the terms encountered during worship or study. The passages quoted in this essay are from the English Standard Version (ESV) unless otherwise noted. To the best of my abilities, I have tried not to take passages out of context and apply them inappropriately.

The Most Important Word

The Word of God is never mere words.

—Lailah Gifty Akita

We must begin by asking, what is the most important word of all? The answer to that question forms the basis for everything else. There appears to be only one answer to the question. That is the *Word of God* or simply the *Word*. Lutherans believe that the *Bible* is the Word of God. The Bible has been called a book of books because it comprises sixty-six individual books written by many different authors who lived at widely separated times in history. Lutherans also believe that those authors were *inspired* and *guided by God*, as they wrote the texts. According to its own testimony in a passage from the book of 2 Timothy, "All Scripture is *breathed out* by God and profitable for teaching, for reproof, for correction, and for training in righteousness, that the man of God may be complete, equipped for every good work" (2 Timothy 3:16). Sometimes, the word *canon* is used to describe this collection of sacred writings. The term refers to the collection of writings accepted as *inspired by God* that the church regards as comprising *Scripture*.

How each of the books was considered to have been inspired by God, judged authoritative, and included in the Bible is a long and fascinating story far beyond the scope of this essay. A list of the books included in the Bible is given in the front of any copy of the Bible.

The praise team at my church has sung the song "Seek Ye First" (LSB 712) many times, which emphasizes an important truth.

The second verse of the song is a slightly reworded passage from Deuteronomy, another of the books of the Bible, that reads in part, "That he [God] might make you know that man does not live by bread alone, but man lives by every word that comes from the mouth of the LORD" (Deuteronomy 8:3). That is a definite and interesting statement. But who of us has heard the physical voice of God speaking directly to us? I would venture to say that none of us have. Yet we have heard the Word of God as pastors and lectors speak or as we read the words written by the inspired authors of the Bible.

This might be a good time to consider a question that perplexed me for some years. Why do we speak of the Word of God rather than the Words of God? The Bible contains many words and records numerous instances when God spoke directly to or through his servants. The answer is that the Bible is a coherent and focused whole. It reveals God's will and his plan to rescue the human race from sin and eternal death. Its central teaching is the person *Jesus* and his saving work. Incidentally, his name means "the Lord is salvation" or, more directly, "he saves." There is much more to say about other words that describe the structure and content of this marvelous document in a later section.

However, beyond the written and spoken word, there is another striking and powerful reference to the Word in the book of John. John writes, "In the beginning was the Word and the Word was with God and the Word was God. He was in the beginning with God" (John 1:1–2). John then goes on through eleven more verses hinting at and providing clues to the identity of this Word who was with God throughout eternity. Then, in verse 14, he pulls the trigger and states, "And the Word became flesh and dwelt among us, and we have seen his glory, glory as of the only Son from the Father, full of grace and truth." This is a clear and direct reference to the Jesus of history who was born and lived among us for some thirty years. In these passages, *Jesus* is equated with God and called the *Living Word*!

Not only does this passage point to Jesus and equates him with God, but also it contains what is perhaps the most consoling word from the Word—*grace*. Grace is the incomprehensible quality or attribute of God that moves him in Christ to give great and precious gifts to us though we are unworthy. He provides our food and clothing, intellect and abilities, relationships with family and friends, the forgiveness of sins, and eternal life. It is often said that "God is love." That is true but passive. He also loves. Grace is the visible expression of his love in action (Figure 2). Each day, we experience his love as we receive these undeserved gifts that maintain, nourish, and strengthen us.

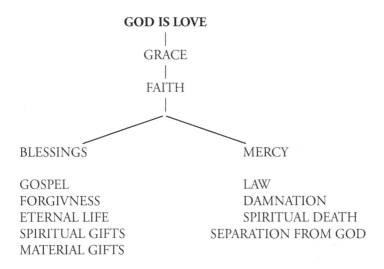

Figure 2. Grace through Faith is God's love in action

The familiar old hymn, "Amazing Grace," explains our indebtedness in the third verse, "His grace has brought me safe thus far. His grace will lead me home" (LSB 744:3). A newer song, "Grace Alone," sometimes sung by my congregation's praise team accurately states that as we pass God's love to others, it is only by grace that there is any success. God's grace gives meaning to all the other words and defines his relationship with us. The word occurs frequently in the Bible. Watch for it in the passages quoted throughout this work. It is fundamental and comforting.

Some Words of Worship

So here I am to worship.
Here I am to bow down.
Here I am to say that
You're my God.

—Tim Hughes, Here I Am to Worship

Now that we agree on what the Word is, we are ready to consider words from it or related to the worship of our great God. Individuals are brought to Christianity in different ways. Some of us are life-long Christians taught and brought to church by our parents. Some are invited by a friend or are attracted by radio, TV, or the Internet. Others develop interest by reading the Bible or religious literature. A few might take the daunting action of contacting a pastor or venturing into a church on a Sunday morning. The last two are more serious obstacles than most of us would like to believe. In spite of these differences, whether in a traditional or contemporary worship setting, sooner or later, everyone encounters terms or concepts that are unfamiliar or perplexing.

Let's begin with the basics and consider the gathering of Christians on a Sunday morning in a church building. A popular song titled "Here I Am to Worship" is sung by many congregations and praise choirs. What does the word *worship* mean in this context? Is it the same as saying, "I worship the ground that you walk on," or "My kids just worship that baseball player or Hollywood star?" Among several definitions, my dictionary defines worship as "an act or ceremony of showing reverence and adoration." That's not quite what we are looking for because we can also show reverence and respect to our president, governor, or any dignitary. Another definition adds: "To pay *divine* honors." We are familiar with that word. We sometimes say, "That's simply divine," or "It is such a divine outfit." However, *divine* does not mean really nice; it means belonging to or having the nature of God. It means something sacred. That is something very different than nice clothes or a memorable song. Therefore, the ceremony, the worship service, which takes place in a Christian church, is a *divine worship service*. It is focused on Jesus and designed to enrich and strengthen our faith. It is the gathering of Christians during which God provides and we hear his Word, receive his body and blood in the sacrament to assure us that our sins have been forgiven, and finally are given his blessing to return to workaday lives. We respond to these gifts with thanks and praise. In other words, God is the prime actor in the service, not us.

A traditional divine Christian worship service is conducted according to a prescribed form or set of forms that guide, structure, and order the flow and sequence of public religious worship. That text or guide is called the *order of service* or the *Liturgy*. There usually are several different orders of service in hymnals and service books. In the Lutheran Service Book (2006) commonly used in the Lutheran Church Missouri Synod, they are termed *Settings* and labeled *Divine Service Settings One through Five* and can be used alternately to provide variety to the worship experience. Other orders of service are designed for special occasions such as baptisms, funerals, and weddings. Chapters 27 and 28 of Lutheranism 101 provide an excellent discussion of the pattern and meaning of the divine worship service that will not be duplicated here. A short summary is in order, however. The major sections of the liturgy are as follows: the *Preparation*, which includes public acknowledgment of our sins and the recognition that they have been forgiven; the *Service of the Word* with readings and lessons from and about God's Word; sometimes the *Service of the Sacrament*; and a closing, *Blessing*, all surrounded and supported with music. Sacraments will be addressed in a later section. The Settings are further divided into sections based on long-standing practice and tradition. The heading of each section is in Latin, Greek, or Hebrew words that appear unusual and foreign to a modern worshiper. For example, the Nunc Dimittis, meaning the Song of Simeon that he sang when the baby Jesus was presented at the temple in Jerusalem.

Many Christians cherish the long-used and familiar liturgies, whereas others view them as too prescriptive and limiting and therefore prefer a more modern less structured form of worship. Following the guidance of a Setting during worship can be confusing, even intimidating, to visitors or new Christians because of the instructions to stand, sit, kneel, pray, or respond. Contemporary worship guides usually do not use the traditional headings, and the divine service is more free-flowing and even spontaneous. However, the framework of the service remains. Music is an important and often active component of worship. Whatever our preference, traditional or contemporary worship style, the service is not about us. It is not about what songs we like to sing, how animated we are, how we like the pastor to dress, or what types of sermons we want to hear. We must always remember that the divine service is about Jesus and his saving work.

During a worship service, a casual visitor or guest, along with members of the congregation, will hear, read, or speak some apparently familiar words. However, there are words used during a divine worship service that deserve greater consideration from long-time Christians as well as novices. These words are familiar because we have heard, spoke, or read them before, probably innumerable times, if we regularly attend worship services, and we seem to understand them. But do we?

Let's start with an easy word and consider the familiar word *amen*. This is a word that occurs frequently during worship services, and we have heard it or responded with it many, many times. We also use it after our personal private prayers and often toss it out without thinking much about it; for example, before a meal, we say, "Thank you, Lord, for this food we are about to receive. Amen." We also use the word quite casually when we say, "Amen! I'm glad that is finally over!" For a long time, I thought that it meant the end—that the prayer is over and I was done asking, thanking, or praising, usually asking. That is not the case. It does signal that a prayer is over, but it means much more than that. It actually is a Hebrew word meaning it is true or certain. "For all the promises of God find their Yes in him [Jesus]. That is why it is through him that we utter our *Amen* to God for his glory" (2 Corinthians 1:20). God has promised to hear our prayers, and his promises are sure. With this word, we signal and confirm our trust in him. Amen! Yes, yes, it shall be so.

The word *holy* is encountered frequently during worship, in readings, hymns, and songs, as well as in other contexts. This is an extremely important word, the significance of which is not fully appreciated by most of us. We might use the word to refer to a book, the Holy Bible, for example. We speak of places such as the Holy Land of Israel. Someone might be said to be a holy man signifying a pious and dedicated person. Another person might say, "Holy cow, that play by the shortstop was amazing!" However, the deeper meaning goes far beyond these common uses. God calls himself holy when he said to Moses, "Speak to all the congregation of the people of Israel and say to them, You shall be holy for I the Lord your God am holy" (Leviticus 19:2). What does it mean to say that God is holy? It means that he is morally and ethically perfect. Holiness is an inherent characteristic of God. That God is holy and perfect, whereas we are not, is a sobering and, for many, a troubling concept. Why do we need to be perfect? If we are honest, we know we cannot be perfect. How can we be as perfect as God requires? If we pursue the answers to these questions on our own, we either lapse into pride—I am good enough and better than most—or into despair, I can never please God and am worthless. Later we will explore words that explain how a holy God has taken care of this unsettling disconnect between his demand for perfection and our inability to achieve it.

Hosanna is another word that occurs in the order of worship and in hymns and songs. It is an exclamation of welcome and joy meaning "save us now." This welcome was shouted by the people as Jesus made his triumphant entry into Jerusalem on the Sunday before his death. "And those who went before and those who followed were shouting, 'Hosanna! Blessed is he who comes in the name of the Lord'" (Mark 11:9). Because of this, it is commonly associated with Holy Week, the week before Easter, and the hymn "Hosanna,

Loud Hosanna" (LSB 443) is often sung on Palm Sunday, the Sunday before Easter. It is a stirring hymn, of which the first verse says,

> Hosanna, loud hosanna, the little children sang;
> Through pillared court and temple the lovely anthem rang.
> To Jesus who had blessed them, close folded to his breast,
> The children sang their praises, the simplest and the best.

Welcome to Jerusalem, Jesus, King of kings! But beware. People are fickle, and bad things are about.

The exclamation *alleluia* also occurs frequently in the divine service and in hymns and songs and means "Praise the LORD!" It is the Greek form of the Hebrew word *hallelujah*. We might use both forms informally in other situations, such as, "Alleluia! George has finally finished that overdue report!" or "Hallelujah! Now you see what I mean about Ted!" During worship, it is said or sung in praise, thanksgiving, or acclamation to the LORD. It is perhaps most familiar to many in the Easter morning greeting that Christians have used for centuries: "Christ has risen!" and the response is "He has risen indeed! Alleluia!" It is also joyously sung in the Easter hymn "Jesus Christ is Risen Today" (LSB 457), the third verse of which says,

> But the pains which he endured, Alleluia!
> Our salvation have procured, Alleluia!
> Now above the sky He's king, Alleluia!
> Where the angels ever sing, Alleluia!

In most versions of the Bible, halleluiah or alleluia occurs only in Revelation 19 where it appears several times. The chorus of the modern song "Sometimes Alleluia" provides the more commonly rendered translation, "Praise the LORD." That is the usual translation as it is in the Psalms. Praise the LORD, all nations! Extol him, all peoples! For great is his steadfast love toward us, and the faithfulness of the LORD endures forever. Praise the LORD! (Psalm 117:1–2)

Glory is a little word loaded with meaning. In fact, it has several meanings. It has already appeared in several places earlier. We often use it in a somewhat pedestrian manner such as when we attempt to describe the beauty of an evening sunset by saying it is glorious. If we try to express the features and effects of that phenomenon, words fail. What we see and feel is beyond our ability to describe adequately. "Wow" or "That's amazing" are the most we can say. In another instance, armies and sport teams sometimes have "glorious" victories. Those are great and special occurrences. They fill us with pride and provide a rush of adrenaline. We are fired up!

Glory is used often in our worship services in the sense of the praise by which we honor God. A well-known Christmas carol repeats the refrain, "Hark! The herald angels sing, 'Glory to the newborn King!'" (LSB 380). A praise band song "Glory to God Forever" in a similar way encourages us to sing glory to God forever! There are others of each type that express our joyful adoration of our God. We are encouraged if not commanded to do so for the Scriptures say, "Shout for joy to God, all the earth; sing the glory of his name; give to him glorious praise!" (Psalm 66:1–2) But be careful here. In contrast to our favorite sport hero being named MVP by a vote of fans or players or General Jones receiving a fifth star and another medal from the army high command or the government, nothing that we do gives or adds to God's stature. We are simply recognizing his overwhelming greatness.

In contemporary worship praise songs such as "Glory to God forever" substitute for "Gloria in Excelsis" meaning glory to God in the highest of the more formal liturgy, whereas praise songs well render our honor to God, "Gloria in Excelsis" also depicts another meaning of glory. Although it appears in somewhat different forms in the settings in the Lutheran Service Book, I think that the version in Setting Four most clearly makes the distinction on page 204. This introduces something very different—the *glory of God*. The first verse reads,

> To God on high be glory and peace to all the earth;
> Good-will from God in heaven Proclaimed at Jesus's birth!
> We praise and bless you, Father; your holy name we sing.
> Our thanks for your great *glory*, Lord God our heavenly King.

So what is the glory of God? That's not an easy question to answer. First, let's try this: it is an intrinsic quality of God's greatness and power. We struggle to comprehend the enormity of it. Our understanding is limited. It is somewhat like describing that sunset that almost everyone has seen. The psalmist notes, "The heavens declare the glory of God, and the sky above proclaims his handiwork" (Psalm 19:1). Words are inadequate to fully describe the concept, but that passage provides a hint. In the Old Testament, God's glory is often described as a cloud or consuming fire that led or prevented the Israelites from traveling during their exodus from Egypt. Moses once said, "Please show me your glory" (Exodus 33:18). Amazingly, God granted his request, but he secured Moses in a large crack in the rock and shielded his eyes because he said, "You cannot see my face, for man shall not see me and live" (Exodus 33:20). In New Testament times, men did see his glory and lived and will live eternally because of it. "He [Jesus] is the radiance of the glory of God and the exact imprint of his nature, and he upholds the universe by the word of his power" (Hebrews 1:3). Does this fully explain God's glory and majesty? No, but it should humble us.

These words are part of most if not all divine worship services. They are certainly familiar to those of us who frequently attend services even if we do not pay much attention or completely comprehend their significance. They are words that even non-Christians vaguely recognize, and they might be among the first words new

Christians or those not yet Christians hear or read as they struggle to make sense of a budding faith or to satisfy their religious curiosity during a visit to a church. While these words might stand at the door of faith for some or form part of the heart of faith for mature Christians, their meanings are derived from God's Word, and they are applied in the divine service.

Words Pertaining to the Structure of the Bible

A classic is a book that has never finished saying what it has to say.

—Italo Calvino

Although Italo Calvino was not a Christian, this quote applies perfectly. The Bible, that fabulous book, provides more insights and understanding each time it is read and studied. It may be divided in a number of ways, but the major divisions are the *Old Testament*, of thirty-nine separate books written before Jesus was born, and the *New Testament*, of twenty-seven separate books written after Jesus died and rose. Except for a few passages, the Old Testament was written in the Hebrew language and the New Testament in Greek. One of the strengths of the Lutheran tradition is that pastors are familiarized and that some delve into those languages. Over the years, the Bible has been translated into more than a thousand languages and many *versions*. A version is a particular translation, phrasing, and interpretation of the text. For many years, the King James Version was widely used. That translation, first published in 1611, is written in older-style English. It uses terms such as "thee," "thou," and "thine," which are difficult to read for some but sound poetical to others. Since most people are at least somewhat familiar with the story of David and Goliath, let's look at a short passage to illustrate the differences. The King James translation of 1 Samuel 17:46 reads,

"This day will the LORD deliver thee into mine hand, and I will smite thee and take thine head from thee." In the English Standard Version, the passage says, "This day the LORD will deliver you into my hand, and I will strike you down and cut off your head." Both translations say the same thing but in very different ways.

So, why is the Bible divided into the Old and the New Testaments? It is much more than because some of the books are older than others. The word *testament* can have several meanings. Perhaps we are most familiar with its use in the context of a person's solemn final wishes, as in "last will and testament." In the biblical application, it can best be translated as *covenant.* A covenant is an agreement between two parties (Lockyer, 1986, p 259). You enter into a type of covenant when you sign a contract to buy a different car or recite wedding vows. However, in the Bible, a covenant has a broader meaning than a simple contract. A contract has a specified end date and involves only one or a few elements. You might agree to make payments of $250 each month for forty-eight months for your new vehicle. A biblical covenant refers to a permanent all-encompassing agreement between God and men. Furthermore, it must be noted that when such a covenant was established, God was always the initiator, not humans. God proposed the requirements and set the expectations. During the Old Testament times, God entered into a number of covenants with individuals separately and with the Hebrew people collectively none of which endured because the humans involved were unable or unwilling to fulfill the conditions of the agreements. Speaking to them, God said through the prophet Hosea, "But like Adam they transgressed the covenant; there they dealt faithlessly with me (Hosea 6:7). The covenant of the New Testament is founded on Jesus and is sure. We need to look further at this amazing book and the details of God's plan for his people.

The Old Testament

Holy words long preserved
For our walk in this world
They resound with God's own heart
Oh let the ancient words impart

—Lynn DeShazo, "Ancient Words"

The thirty-nine books of the Old Testament can be subdivided into several groups. The first five books were written by Moses and known as the *Pentateuch* and sometimes referred to as the *Torah* or the *Book of the Law*. In those five books, among other things, God set out specific guidelines and expectations for his chosen people, the Hebrew nation—most notably the *Ten Commandments* (Appendix 1). God commanded Moses to write down all the laws for the people, and God himself wrote the *Ten Commandments* on two stone tablets. "And he [God] gave to Moses, when he had finished speaking with him on Mount Sinai, the two tablets of the *testimony*, tablets of stone, written with the finger of God" (Exodus 31:18). The Ten Commandments are the very foundation of God's Law. Beyond the Ten Commandments, in the Pentateuch, God established moral, civil, and ceremonial codes that ordered every aspect of the lives of his chosen people Israel (Appendix 2).

Leviticus and Deuteronomy, two of the books of the Pentateuch, present an exhaustive list of examples of do's and don'ts decreed by God to be obeyed. The list of laws is long and specific. Perhaps the *Law* can be summarized in this way: "You shall therefore love the

Lord your God and keep his charge, his statutes, his rules, and his commandments always" (Deuteronomy 11:1). That is a simple straight forward statement: just be dedicated to being perfect! That is, be holy! How is this possible? We have considered what it means to be holy—to be morally and ethically perfect. In addition, God is also *righteous*, that is, he is always just and does the right thing. "But the LORD of hosts is exalted in justice, and the Holy God shows himself holy in righteousness" (Isaiah 5:16). Again, God is perfect in righteousness and is set apart. He is fundamentally different from humans, yet in the Law, he demands us to be like him—perfect and righteous. These are tough, no impossible requirements! The specific lists of rules given in the Pentateuch are long and the details overwhelming. While it is somewhat comforting to learn that in these New Testament times, we are no longer bound by the Old Testament ceremonial and civil codes, the Ten Commandments remain as God's model for a holy life. We have no possibility of keeping and fulfilling the Law perfectly on our own. We will always fall short. There is more to say about that and our inability to keep the Law coming up.

The following twelve books of *Historical Writings* cover the story of the Hebrews, God's chosen people. The historical books provide a narrative of the struggles of those people to worship and obey God as he commanded and their frequent failures to remain separate from surrounding nations, follow his requirements, and fulfill his expectations. There are many lessons to be learned from those historical books. The next five books are called *Wisdom Writings*, or *Poetical Books*. The Wisdom Books seek to show that it is God's wisdom, not man's, that is supreme and that humans should be humble before God in reverence and obedience. A vivid example of the supremacy of God's wisdom occurs in the later chapters of the book of Job as Job and his friends struggle to understand the severe troubles that have befallen him. He and his friends have each attempted to explain Job's misfortunes and questioned God's actions and motives. God then settles the issue when he answered Job and his friends as well saying, "Who is this that darkens counsel by words without knowledge? Dress for action like a man; I will question you, and you make it known to me. Where were you when I laid the foundation of the earth? Tell me, if you have understanding. Who determined its measurements—surely you know!" (Job 38:2–5). God then goes on to provide a humbling list of things beyond man's abilities and understanding that he created and controls. This is wisdom that we all can use.

The *Prophetical Books* are separated into five long books written by the *major prophets* and the twelve shorter books of the *minor prophets*. The messages of the minor prophets are no less important or significant; their books are just; yes, that's right, shorter. During the Old Testament times, *prophets* were men who were *called by God*, that is, they were summoned and appointed directly by God. As he said to the prophet Jeremiah, "Before I formed you in the womb I knew you, and before you were born I *consecrated* you; I appointed you a prophet to the nations" (Jeremiah 1:5). Prophets were *consecrated*, set aside, for a special purpose. Today many church bodies still consider their invitations to individuals to serve as pastors and professional church workers in their congregations and schools as *divine calls*. A prophet received not only his appointment or call from God but also his words. When Jeremiah protested that he was just a youth and did not know how to speak, he received this answer: "Then the LORD put out his hand and touched my mouth. And the LORD said to me, 'Behold, I have put my words in your mouth'" (Jeremiah 1:9). That is another passage that clearly shows that the Scriptures were inspired by God. Today, we usually think of a prophet as someone who supposedly can see the future. Although Old Testament prophets sometimes predicted future events, more importantly, they were charged to warn the people and encourage them to forsake their godless behavior and turn from their sins. These men were not unengaged dreamers who sat on the sidelines waiting for people to come their way for advice. Prophets spoke for God at his command and communicated his messages that served to teach and correct the people who had often gone badly astray. The role of a prophet was a contentious and often dangerous one. They were often directed to challenge the kings, princes, and religious leaders of their day and to speak against the cultural decay of their times. While some prophets wrote down their messages and their books are included in the Bible, some did not but are known only from the writings of others.

The New Testament

Words of life, words of hope
Give us strength, help us cope
In this world where e'er we roam
Ancient words will guide us home

—Lynn DeShazo, "Ancient Words"

The New Testament can also be subdivided and the twenty-seven books placed into groups based on common content and purpose. The first four books are referred to as the *gospels*. The gospels are the basis of the Christian religion and focus on Jesus's time on earth. The word *gospel* is used in two primary ways. In one use, it refers to one of those first four books of the New Testament written by Matthew, Mark, Luke, and John. The four books tell the story of Jesus's life and work from somewhat different perspectives. Therefore, for example, we might hear or read, "The gospel according to Matthew" or "The gospel lesson today is from Luke." More importantly, it refers to the message of those books that is the *good news* of what God has done for us through Jesus. Each of the authors, in his own way, recounts the life and *ministry*, that is the teachings of Jesus; however, they are not complete biographies as they focus mainly on his work and message during the last few years of his life.

The other books of the New Testament affirm and explain the truths now accepted by the Christian Church. The book of Acts is considered a sequel to the Gospel of Luke and is a history of the early church. Acts documents the spread of Christianity throughout the

Roman Empire. The following twenty-one books called *Epistles* are letters written by leaders of the early church to instruct, correct, and further the spiritual growth of congregations established by their missionary activities. The final book of the New Testament, *Revelation*, is *apocalyptic* in style. That is, it was written to reveal, among other things, religious mysteries and deals with the coming end times. All the books of the New Testament were written after Jesus lived.

Words of Promise

Every word of God proves true.

—Proverbs 30:5

Old Testament Covenants
and Promises from God

Ancient words ever true
Changing me and changing you
We have come with open hearts
Let the ancient words impart

—Lynn DeSazo, "Ancient Words"

In the Old Testament, God made several promises and established far-reaching covenants with individuals and with the Hebrew people. Foremost of these individuals was the *patriarch*, Abraham, who is considered the father of the Hebrew nation. *Patriarchs* were tribal leaders who lived before the time of the great prophet Moses. These men were prominent figures in the history of the Hebrew nation whom God guided and spoke to in some amazing ways. An important and instructive example of a covenant between God and a human is recorded in Genesis, the first book of the Bible. There God said to Abraham, "I will surely bless you, and I will surely multiply your offspring as the stars of heaven and as the sand that is on the sea-shore. And your offspring shall possess the gate of his enemies, and in your offspring shall all the nations of the earth be blessed, because you have obeyed my voice" (Genesis 22:17–18). Although there are some slight variations in the translations in different versions of the Bible, this passage is striking for two reasons. First, God refers to Abraham's offspring in two ways. In the plural, it is a promise of the formation of the Hebrew nation. In the singular, it is taken as a clear reference to and a promise of the *Messiah* to come. The *Messiah* was long anticipated by the Jews who believed that he would be the *Anointed One* sent from God to save his people. In Old Testament times, a man was *anointed* by pouring oil on his head to signify that he was selected or set apart that is consecrated for a special office or purpose. Many, perhaps most, Jews of Old Testament times longed for a Messiah who would be a strong political leader and who would establish a great earthly kingdom and return Israel to a position of prominence among the nations. Second, his promise that "all nations will be blessed" indicated that the *Gentiles* as well as the Jews would be included in Gods' kingdom. Gentiles are not of the Jewish race and therefore were not considered members of God's chosen people. The Jews often avoided and looked down upon the Gentiles. Today, most Christians are Gentiles. Thank God for this fulfilled promise!

One of the most significant covenants of the Old Testament was established with the Hebrew nation and the great *prophet Moses* who led the people during the *Exodus*, which was their flight and escape from slavery and oppression in Egypt. With the *covenant of Mount Sinai*, God gave the Law to his people through Moses. *Mount Sinai* is a mountain somewhere in what is now the Sinai Peninsula of northeastern Egypt. Its exact location is uncertain. The Hebrew people were camped near the mountain waiting for Moses to consult with God for further instructions. There God spoke directly to Moses saying, "Now therefore, if you will indeed obey my voice and keep my covenant, you shall be my treasured possession among all peoples, for all the earth is mine and you shall be to me a kingdom of priests and a holy nation. These are the words that you shall speak to the people of Israel" (Exodus 19:5–6). When Moses brought these words of promise to the people, "All the people answered together and said, 'All that the LORD has spoken we will do'" (Exodus 19:8). With these words, the Israelites agreed to and affirmed the covenant. In this instance, in spite of all that God had done for them, the Israelites broke the covenant by idol worship even before Moses returned from Mount Sinai with the stone tablets and the covenant had to be reinstituted. God is faithful, does not break his covenants, and keeps his promises, while history has shown that humans are weak and often fail to carry out their part of the bargain—a reoccurring theme throughout the Old Testament. In spite of all this, God also said, "I, I am he who blots out your transgressions for my own sake, and I will not remember your sins" (Isaiah 43:25). Here is a clear passage of pure grace and gospel. This statement might come as a surprise because many people think that the Old Testament presents only the terror of a wrathful God, while the New Testament presents the comfort of a forgiving God through Christ. That is not the case. When Jesus refers to the Scriptures as he often did, he is speaking of the Old Testament as the New Testament did not exist. "You search the Scriptures because you think that in them you have eternal life: and it is they that bear witness about me (John 5:39).

The New Covenant of the New Testament

Holy words of our faith
Handed down to this age
Came to us through sacrifice
Oh hear the faithful words of Christ

—Lynn DeSazo, "Ancient Words"

In the New Testament, which means *new covenant*, God promises a new relationship with him based on his new and better promises. That a new covenant was to replace the old was foretold in the Old Testament by the prophet Jeremiah. He states, "*Behold*, the days are coming, declares the LORD, when I will make a new covenant with the house of Israel and the house of Judah" (Jeremiah 31:31). In the New Testament, that entire passage is quoted in Hebrews 8:8–12. Jeremiah used the important attention-grabbing word *behold*. When we read the word *behold* or hear it as a passage of Scripture is read, we should take special notice. It is the equivalent of the modern "Listen up!" which I frequently heard during my time in the army. It occurs in many passages throughout the Bible, and its purpose is to focus our thoughts. It is an alert sign that says, stop, and pay attention because there is something important or significant coming. It is often used when God is speaking directly to someone as he was to Jeremiah. It is also sometimes associated with the appearance of the heavenly messengers known as *angels* (Appendix 3). When the *Archangel Gabriel*, an angel of high rank, appeared to Mary to foretell the birth of Jesus, he several times used the word to emphasize the importance of his message (Luke 1:26–38). The prediction in the Old Testament of a new covenant to come and the announcement of the birth of Jesus in the New Testament are significant events that we should indeed behold.

A new covenant was necessary because humans are incapable of being completely faithful to their promises and fulfilling the requirements of God's Law. "For if that first covenant had been faultless, there would have been no occasion to look for a second" (Hebrews 8:7). We are weak, anti-God, and sinful. *Sin* is any action, thought, word, or attitude that does not meet the standards set by God. To paraphrase a *Planters Peanut* commercial, "God takes sin very seriously!" The prophet Isaiah points this out vividly saying, "But your *iniquities* have made a separation between you and your God, and your sins have hidden his face from you so that he does not hear (Isaiah 59:2). The word *iniquity*, which means wickedness or lack of moral principles, sometimes is used to amplify the seriousness of sin. Yet, we don't need to commit a horrific crime or be a notorious villain to arouse God's wrath. We have seen that God's standard is nothing less than continuous and perfect obedience, that is, holiness—not "I have done pretty well," not "I tried my best," and not "I sin less than other people."

Here is an example. Suppose you are driving on a highway on which the speed limit is 65 miles per hour. It is a beautiful morning, and because you are not in any hurry, your cruise control is set right on the speed limit. As you approach a small town on a wide boulevard, the speed limit drops to 25 miles per hour, so you decrease your speed to 30. A minute or two later, a vehicle zooms past traveling much faster than you are. Shaking your head, you remark to your passenger, "Some drivers pay no attention to speed limit signs. He should get a ticket." The question is who broke the law? In most instances, it is unlikely that the police will stop you for driving 5 miles over the posted speed limit, but you both are lawbreakers. The hard truth is one little slip in any way will get you in deep trouble. "For whoever keeps the whole law but fails at one point has become accountable for all of it" (James 2:10). We have all done it. We have each slipped in many ways, both big and small. Because everyone *transgresses* or violates the law many times in many ways, we cannot be delivered from the power of sin by obeying the law. We do not relish being called *transgressors* or lawbreakers, but in reality, that is what we are. The thought that we are lost in sin is not something that we like to hear or easily accept. In spite of our discomfort, the Scriptures make it impossible to wiggle out from under that verdict. "If we say that we have no sin, we deceive ourselves and the truth is not in us" (1 John 1:8). That is a pretty direct statement. God is holy! God hates sin! We are all sinners! Therefore, if justice is to prevail, we are doomed! If we consider this for even a moment, the reality seems overwhelming, and we are helpless. If we depend on our own efforts to fulfill the Law, we will be *condemned*, that is, declared guilty, held accountable for our sins, and consigned to everlasting damnation. We will be separated from God, and he will turn his face away from us. That is quite a dilemma.

This all seems hopeless and discomforting. But there is hope! God hates sin but loves the sinner. We learn the bright side to this equation when we look more closely at this new covenant and the new promise God has for the human race. But first, let's be clear about one thing: God must and did make the first move. "For there is one God, and there is one mediator between God and men, the man *Christ Jesus*" (1 Timothy 2:5). Christ is not a second or a family name like Anderson or Smith; rather it is a Greek term for the long-awaited *Messiah*, or the *Anointed One*, prophesized in the Old Testament. Jesus is plainly recognized as the Messiah by the Apostle Peter when in response to this question, Jesus addressed to his disciples, "And he [Jesus] asked them, 'But who do you say that I am?' Peter answered him, 'You are the Christ'" (Mark 8:29). Christians consider Jesus the Messiah who came not to found a powerful earthly kingdom and return Israel to prominence among nations, but to save humans from their sins and to establish a heavenly kingdom.

Words of Eternal Life

"Lord, to whom should we go? You have the words of eternal life."

—John 6:68

Consider what God has done for us through Jesus. First, God sent Jesus into history to bring us a clear statement of the gospel and to establish the new covenant. The Apostle Peter wrote, "He was foreknown before the foundation of the world but was made *manifest* [that is revealed and made clearly visible] in the last times for the sake of you" (1 Peter 1:20). Jesus came for us! Through him, we have a glimpse of our God as Paul further explains, "He [Jesus] is the image of the invisible God, the firstborn of all creation" (Colossians 1:15). Second, Jesus fulfilled the demands of the Law for us. He said of himself, "Do not think that I have come to abolish the Law or the Prophets; I have not come to abolish them but to fulfill them" (Matthew 5:17). Thanks be to God! He accomplished something that we never could! Finally, Jesus paid a terrible price in our place for our sins. He assumed the punishment that should be yours and mine.

How can we tap into Christ's work, gain the benefits, and receive *salvation*? That is the deliverance from the power of sin. How do we obtain *forgiveness* or pardon from God and can we be assured of eternal life in spite of our shortcomings? In some way, we must have been brought together with God, and the separation from him ended. Many of us might have a family member or friend to whom, for some reason, we have not spoken for years. The relationship is broken. However, if we extend or receive a kind offer to forgive and forget, it is a pleasure to reestablish the former connection. That process of returning to the right relationship with another is *reconciliation*. Above all, we need to be *reconciled* to God. With a friend or relative, the reconciliation may be initiated by either of us. Either one of us can reach out and begin the process of restoring the former relationship. That is not how our sin-broken relationship with God is repaired. Restoration of a right relationship with God depends entirely on him, not on us. What then is the cure? Paul states the remedy, "All this is from God, who through Christ reconciled us to himself and gave us the ministry of reconciliation; that is, in Christ God was reconciling the world to himself, not counting their trespasses against them, and entrusting to us the message of reconciliation" (2 Corinthians 5:18–19). Jesus stepped up in our stead, satisfied God's holy and just wrath with our sins, accepted the punishment that we deserve for our sins, and rendered full satisfaction for them by his life and sacrificial death. This is the act of *atonement*, which reconciled us to God and restored unity with him. Jesus Christ *atoned* for our sins by fulfilling the law and taking on the punishment that should be ours.

The Jewish religious and political officials of his day considered Jesus a threat. Perhaps they were worried that he would usurp their positions as national leaders. Perhaps they were concerned about an uprising of the people. Perhaps they thought that their relationship with the Romans was in jeopardy. Perhaps it was all three and more, but in any case, they had him arrested and taken before the *Sanhedrin*, the highest court of justice of the Jewish people at that time for what was really a shame trial. There he was accused of *blasphemy*, which is showing contempt and lack of reverence for God. Because the Jews were dominated by Rome, they could not legally execute anyone; therefore, he was sent to *Pontus Pilate*, the Roman governor. Pilate yielded to pressure from the Jewish leaders, and Jesus was put to death by Roman soldiers. Jesus died by *crucifixion*, which was employed by different people of the ancient world but was perfected and widely used by the Romans to punish the worst criminals and deter rebellion. Being nailed to a large wooden cross is a slow and painful way to die. However, without the next astounding event, Jesus's *resurrection* on Easter Sunday, there would be no good news— no gospel. By raising Jesus from death, God affirmed that he is Christ, the world's *Redeemer*, and that his sacrifice was accepted. Because of his death, we receive *redemption*. We have been *redeemed*—ransomed or bought with a price. And what a price it was. Jesus's death freed us from the payment demanded by a righteous God for our sin. Forty days following his resurrection and after appearing bodily to his disciples and many others, his *ascension* into heaven ended his physical presence on earth. "While he blessed them, he parted from them and was carried up into heaven" (Luke 24:51). Though we will die one day, in Christ's resurrection and ascension, we are assured of his second coming and our own resurrection.

Let's look at this from another angle. Suppose that someone is dishonest and in some way defrauded people of a significant amount of money. The person is arrested, placed in jail, and eventually brought before a judge. The trial is swift. The judge orders the person to jail and to pay restitution. Let us also suppose that the person has a very rich uncle who loves him dearly. This rich uncle not only pays the fine but also reimburses those that were harmed by the actions of his relative. In effect, the person has been redeemed from the consequences of his actions and of the judgment of the court and is free. However, the payment has no lasting value for when the person again defrauded someone; he was arrested and prosecuted again. This time, the outcome is the prison. Thankfully, God did not stop at that point but rather went a step further and declared us not guilty forever. "For there is no distinction: for all have sinned and fall short of the glory of God, and are *justified* by his grace as a gift, through the redemption that is in Christ Jesus" (Romans 3:22–24). We are justified or made right with God through Jesus's life, death, and resurrection. *Justification* is the forgiveness that Jesus claimed for all and that he offers to us in the gospel. By his sinless life and sacrificial death, he paid the required price with the result that God declared the whole world to be *righteous* that is without fault. We are seen as righteous by God through the righteousness of Jesus. "For our sake he [God] made him [Jesus] to be sin who knew no sin, so that in him we might become the righteousness of God" (2 Corinthians 5:21). We will sin again, but our sentence has already been commuted. W. D. Mueller (2016) considers that "justification is the core of the gospel's message." In the pamphlet *Distinctive Doctrines and Customs of the Lutheran Church*, Geo. Luecke writes, "It is the chief doctrine of the Christian religion. It is the great central doctrine of Christianity" (Luecke, p. 14).

How does this work? How do we partake of the justification that Christ has won for us? What do we need to do to be saved? These questions have been asked innumerable times by innumerable people throughout history. That question was asked and answered in the city of Philippi where Paul and a man named Silas were in prison for preaching the gospel and casting out a demon from a slave woman. That night, an earthquake shook the prison. The doors were opened, and the prisoners were released from their shackles. The jailer, fearing that prisoners had escaped, was about to kill himself when he was stopped by Paul's assurance that everyone was still there. "Then he [the jailor] brought them out and said, 'Sirs, what must I do to be saved?' And they said, '*Believe* in the Lord Jesus and you will be saved, you and your household'" (Acts 16:30–31). The answer then is that we need to and can do nothing. We cannot satisfy the law, nor can we do enough good to appease God. "For by grace you have been saved through faith. And this is not your own doing: it is the gift of God, not a result of *works* [deeds], so that no one may boast (Ephesians 2:8–9). This is another precious gift from God by his grace received through faith in Jesus by believing that he is our savior. In the Old Testament, God said, "But the righteous live by his faith" (Habakkuk 2:4). In this sense, *faith* is a complete trust that God will do what he has promised and that his love endures forever.

Atonement, reconciliation, redemption, and justification—these processes have been completed through God's grace by the life, sacrificial crucifixion, and the resurrection of Jesus Christ. However, there is one other process that is not complete and will be ongoing for each of us until death. That is our *sanctification*. "God chose you as the firstfruits to be saved, through sanctification by the Spirit and the belief in the truth" (2 Thessalonians 2:13b). It is another gift of God's grace by which the believer is set apart, freed from the power of sin, and becomes dedicated to God's righteousness. It can be summed up as the Christian's life of faith or Christian living. Unfortunately, our lives are too frequently marked by less than Christian behavior. Sanctification is "the spiritual growth that follows justification by grace through faith in Christ" (Lutheranism 101, p. 84). Sanctification is worked by the Holy Spirit through the *means of grace*: Word and *sacraments*. A *means* is a way by which something is accomplished or a goal attained. A *sacrament* is a sacred act that was instituted by the Lord, contains a visible physical element, and promises forgiveness of sins because of Christ. In the Lutheran Church, there are two sacraments: *baptism* and *Holy Communion*.

The sacrament of *baptism* is the washing with water in the name of the Father, the Son, and the Holy Spirit through which God promises forgiveness of sins and *regeneration*; that is a new life in Christ. "We were buried therefore with him by baptism into death, in order that, just as Christ was raised from the dead by the glory of the Father, we too might walk in the newness of life" (Romans 6:4).

The sacrament of Holy Communion was instituted by Jesus on the evening of his betrayal. "Now as they were eating, Jesus took bread, and after blessing it broke it and gave it to the disciples, and said, 'Take, eat; this is my body.' And he took a cup, and when he had given thanks, he gave it to them saying, 'Drink of it, all of you, for this is my blood of the covenant which is poured out for many for the forgiveness of sins'" (Matthew 26:26–28). Holy Communion assures us that our sins have been forgiven by Christ's sacrifice and is also known as the *Lord's Supper*, the *Sacrament of the Altar*, and other terms.

In reality, our sanctification begins with our *conversion*—the change from being an unbeliever to becoming a believer that Jesus is our Lord and Savior. That turning away from evil and the beginning of faith is the work of the *Holy Spirit*. For some of us, our conversion happened at our baptism. We might not remember a time when we did not consider our self a Christian. For others, that transformation occurred at a specific time or involved a struggle over many years. In spite of God's grace and forgiveness and our efforts to lead a new life of faith and obedience, many times we do not succeed. The process of sanctification is never completed in this life and is often interrupted by our *commission* of sins. We can get better at it throughout our lives, but we still stumble often. Nevertheless, we remain reconciled with God through Christ and are still justified, atoned for, and redeemed.

You might be aware that some of the apostles such as Paul and other important figures in the history of Christianity such as Augustine are called *saints*, as a sign of respect. Commonly, we might consider a *saint* a holy person set apart from the world—who is consecrated to the worship and service of God and known for their important work and prominence in the early Christian church. Sometimes we extend the term such as when we say, "That woman is a saint. She works so hard and helps so many." However, in several Bible passages, we, believers, are called saints as well. For instance, in an Old Testament Psalm, King David wrote, "Sing praise to the LORD, O you his saints, and give thanks to his holy name" (Psalm 30:4). In the New Testament, the Apostle Paul in the introduction to the book of Romans says, "To all those in Rome who are loved by God and called to be saints: Grace to you and peace from God our Father and the Lord Jesus Christ" (Romans 1:7). Not only was he speaking to common living Christian at the time, but also he blessed them with God's grace and peace. To be called saints is a remarkable, even heady designation. One could become puffed up and boastful about being called a saint. But recall that Ephesians 2:8–9 previously quoted cautions that we are saved by grace and not by our status or accomplishments. Personal pride is also excluded by 2 Corinthians 10:17–18, which says, "Let the one who boasts, boast in the Lord. For it is not the one who commends himself who is approved, but the one whom the Lord commends." Each year, the church celebrates *All Saints' Day* on November 1 or on the nearest Sunday. During that worship service, we remember relatives and friends who have died and "are with the saints in heaven."

But again, there seems to be a problem here. We may be called saints, but how does that square with our less than holy behavior?

Once again, God supplies the solution. First, we need to recognize that we are guilty of a multitude of sins that we cannot cover. This is where *confession* comes in. When we *confess* our sins, we acknowledge our sins and take ownership of them realizing that we have done wrong. We may confess privately directly to God, to our pastor or another person, or at a worship service when we make a public and general confession. Not only do we need to confess our sins, but also we must *repent* of them. *Repentance* is a change in our heart and consists of two parts: *contrition* and faith (Wolfmueller, 2016). *Contrition* is sincere sorrow and remorse. If we are not affected by our sins, we are not only "falling short" but also rejecting God's solution to our problem. But contrition without faith can lead down the path to despair. "For godly grief produces a repentance that leads to salvation without regret, whereas worldly grief produces death" (2 Corinthians 7:10). Israel's first king in the Old Testament, Saul, and Judas in the New Testament despaired of forgiveness and took their own life. On the other hand, Israel's next king, David, was guilty of adultery and murder; and the Apostle Peter, who denied Christ, was deeply sorrowful but with faith trusted in God's forgiveness and lived. A beautiful passage in the Old Testament book of Psalms shows the relationship of confession and repentance to God's gift of forgiveness. "I acknowledged my sins to you, and I did not cover [hide] my iniquity; I said, 'I will confess my transgressions to the LORD,' and you forgave the iniquity of my sin" (Psalm 32:5). We are saints because God forgave our sins and accepted Christ's sacrifice as payment for them. In the words of an old spiritual, "When the Saints go marching in," "Oh, Lord I want to be in the number, when the saints go marching in!"

The word confession is also used in the sense of providing testimony of our trust and belief in our Lord Jesus Christ. In this context, confession implies that we will boldly admit and defend our faith in Christ and lead a God-pleasing life to the best of our ability to serve as a model in our community. In this way, we serve as *witnesses* to others. For some reason, *witnessing* or sharing our faith is one of the more difficult things for many of us to do. It is often easy to lapse into silence or avoid situations where we might be challenged. Again, the Lord gives us another encouraging promise to help us at those times; Jesus said, "So everyone who acknowledges me before men, I also will acknowledge before my Father who is in heaven" (Matthew 10:32). We are also provided with strength as Timothy said, "For God gave us a spirit not of fear but of power and love and self-control" (2 Timothy 1:7). Lord, help us to truly believe and accept these encouraging words.

Words of Uncertainty

If you do not know the words, you can hardly know the thing."

—Henry Hazlitt

Have you ever listened to a Sunday morning sermon, heard a reading by a lector, sung a hymn, engaged in a Bible study, or read a passage in the Bible and realize that you don't know what a certain word means? I have been a Christian all my life, a Lutheran Christian to be specific. I have worshipped regularly, attended many Bible study classes, participated in special programs and small groups, and read the Bible and devotional publications. I recite this not as a list of meritorious activities but that in spite of them, like many fellow long-time and practicing Christians, I am often uncertain, sometimes confused, and once in a while more than a little bewildered by the terminology of my faith. Let me share several examples.

The name that a congregation selects for its church not only serves to identify that particular church but also may honor a prominent Christian or represent a Biblical concept that can be less than clear even to members. While there are churches with unusual and modern sounding names, such as Celebration, Living Hope, or Life Bridge, many are named Beautiful Savior, Redeemer, Christ the King, St. Peter, St. Paul, St. John, or St. Mark. The first three of these should now be quite clear, and although we might not know details about the four men honored by many congregations, we realize that they were important in the early Christian Church. Many churches are also called *Zion*, as is the congregation in which I was confirmed and married. But why that name? I never thought much about it. It was just the name of our church. Then one Sunday, our congregation sang the hymn "Lift Up Your Heads, You Everlasting Doors" (LSB 339). I happened to be paying close attention and noticed that in the middle of the first verse there is the phrase, "O Zion's daughter, sing, To greet your coming King." The third verse begins with "Who may ascend Mount Zion's holy hill to do God's will?" *Now that is interesting*, I thought. We have mention of both a daughter and a hill. How do I understand those strikingly different references? I have since learned that the name Zion is derived from a term that has undergone changes in meaning over time and may be applied in a number of ways. It first signified a fortress on a hill at the site of the present city of Jerusalem that long resisted Israel's attempts to capture it. Following its fall to David, Zion was used to designate that hill. By extension, it came to mean Jerusalem, the Holy City, and it is sometimes used to refer to the whole Old Testament Hebrew nation. Modern Christianity employs the term to indicate God's spiritual kingdom, the heavenly Jerusalem. The daughter mentioned in the first verse is the New Testament Christian Church.

On another Sunday, the congregation I now am a member of sang the hymn "Come Thou Fount of Every Blessing" (LSB 686). The first verse is filled with uplifting words such as love, joy, and praise. The second verse, however, opens with "Here I raise my *Ebenezer*, hither by thy help I've come; and I hope by thy good pleasure safely to arrive at home." My mind almost immediately derailed. Ebenezer? Ebenezer? The only Ebenezer that I could think of was good old Ebenezer Scrooge from *A Christmas Carol*—not too likely. It was a head scratcher, and it took me awhile to get back to the remaining verses of the hymn. Later, with some investigation, I learned that the term refers to both a place where the Israelites lost and then twenty years later won battles and to a stone set in place there by the prophet Samuel to commemorate the events. "Then Samuel took a stone and set it up between Mizpah and Shen and called its name Ebenezer, for he said, 'Till now the LORD has helped us'" (1 Samuel 7:12). The name means "stone of help." I had no idea.

Even in well-known and familiar hymns, we encounter and pass by unusual terms. On another Sunday, our congregation sang the familiar hymn "All Hail the Power of Jesus's Name" (LSB 549). Verse 1 reads, "All hail the power of Jesus's name! Let angels prostrate fall; Bring forth the royal *diadem* and crown Him Lord of all. Bring forth the royal diadem and crown Him Lord of all." Now I must admit that I have sung that hymn many times without taking note of that word. So, what is a diadem? It is a distinctive emblem or wrapping on the turban or head dress of a ruler that is worn to signify royal authority and power. The reference is to the royal diadem our Lord wears as the King of kings.

Perhaps a term pops out of a text as we participate in a Bible class or read our Bible or a devotion at home. A word that is not only unfamiliar but also one for which we do not have a clue about its meaning. Here, I am not talking about the many personal and place names that look strange to our eyes and are so difficult to pronounce. Knowing that a term refers to an individual or a location is usually sufficient to understand the passage. Recently, during a men's Bible study of the book of Acts, we came to the passages detailing the selection of seven men to administer the daily work of one of the new Christian congregations to free the leaders to preach. "And what they said pleased the whole gathering and they chose Stephen, a man full of faith and of the Holy Spirit, and Philip, and Prochorus, and Nicanor, and Timon, and Parenas, and Nicolaus, a *proselyte* of Antioch" (Acts 6:5). Some of the names were strange and hard to pronounce but not a problem to understand the importance of the event; however, only a few of the group knew that a proselyte is a convert from one religion or party to another.

On the other hand, it might be a word that we have heard or read before, and even though it was explained to us in the past, it might not be so clear to us when we next encounter it. One evening, as I read the lesson in *Portals of Prayer*, the daily devotional booklet published by the Concordia Press, the passage chosen was 1 John 4:10, "In this is love, not that we have loved God but that He loved us and sent His Son to be the *propitiation* for our sins." Now I knew that I had heard that word before; in fact, I seemed to recall my pastor defining it in a sermon. But what does it mean? Well, propitiation is appeasement or payment. In this passage, propitiation refers to the idea that Jesus died on the cross to satisfy God's just anger and to pay the price God demands for our sins.

On another occasion, I was reading Psalm 45, which is a beautiful description and foretelling of a savior to come and of his powerful rule. Verse 6 says, "Your throne, O God, is forever and ever. The *scepter* of your kingdom is a scepter of uprightness." Again, this is a word that I had seen before, but this time, I took note. What is a scepter, and what does it have to do with God's kingdom? I wrote down the word and a few days later looked it up in a source in the church library. Now I know that it is an elaborately designed staff or rod, a stick if you will, that is a symbol of royal power. The scepter seems to have originated from the staffs carried by early kings and princes who often were shepherds. It is an ornate symbolic object derived from a humble and useful one. In the Psalm passage, it symbolizes power based on God's perfect justice.

To further illustrate my point, consider what often happens when the leader of a Bible class pauses to ask the meaning of a particular word or concept. In another instance, during a study of Genesis, we read the verses containing these words spoken by God to the serpent, "I will put *enmity* between you and the woman, and between your offspring and her offspring" (Genesis 3:15). The leader asked, "What is enmity?" Well, I thought, it can't be good if God put it between the serpent and humans. Members of the group fidgeted a bit uncomfortably, looked intently at the page as if rereading the passage would reveal the answer, or looked blankly at the tabletop waiting for someone else to speak up. Just like it was in your least favorite high school or college class, it was important not to make eye contact with the leader, or you might be called on. Though we had heard the term before, most of us were not confident that we knew its meaning or could coherently explain that the term means hatred or hostility. It is the quality of being enemies.

Common Words with Uncommon Meanings

"When I use a word," Humpty Dumpty said in a
rather scornful tone.
"It means just what I choose it to mean—neither
more nor less."

—Lewis Carroll

Some words are familiar and appear to be easily understood, but we may not appreciate their significance or meaning. For example, hope and fear are common widely used words. We all have hopes and fears in our everyday lives, but what do these words mean in a religious context? Similarly, blessings, mercy, happiness, joy, and peace are widely used words that we often misapply or fail to fully comprehend. If we consider these words more closely, we will appreciate their meanings and find comfort in them.

In the New Testament, Paul wrote, "Therefore, since we have been justified by faith, we have *peace* with God through our Lord Jesus Christ. Through him we have also obtained *access* by faith into this *grace* in which we stand, and we rejoice in *hope* of the glory of God" (Romans 5:1–2). This is an amazing passage chocked full of comfort and promise. The world is constantly searching for peace, but lasting peace among nations is elusive. World War I was touted as the "war to end all wars." How did that work out for us? The peace spoken of here and brought by Christ through his sacrifice and victory over death is between God and humans. We no longer need priests or anyone else to serve as intermediaries because now we have direct access to the Father through Jesus. Therefore, our hope is more than "I hope that it doesn't rain on our picnic" or even more than "I hope that someone will come to rescue me from this flood." Both are uncertain. Our hope is the promised certainty that we have eternal life through faith in Jesus.

Recently, I was looking through the picture and frame section of a large department store that contained many wall and shelf plaques with cute and pithy sayings such as "Love conquers all" and "Friends are gifts from God." One that particularly caught my eye read, "Where there is hope, there is faith." After staring at it and rereading it several times, I realized that the words are backward from what the Word tells us. The author of Hebrews clearly states, "Now faith is the assurance of things hoped for, the conviction of things not seen" (Hebrews 11:1). The plaque should read, "Where there is faith, there is hope." This is God's pledge. "And this is the promise that he made to us—eternal life" (1 John 2:25). God is faithful, holds to his promises, and never lies. In a confirmation service for my nephew that I attended, the pastor said to the confirmands, "The Christian's understanding of hope is not that of the familiar saying "Hope springs eternal, but rather that hope is eternal"—an important and comforting difference. From Jesus, we receive rescue from the power of sin, forgiveness of our own sins, peace with God, and the sure hope of eternal life. Faith is our lifeline through Jesus to eternal life, and his resurrection is hope fulfilled. Faith, justification, peace, and hope all result from God's grace.

We are aware that everyone, even unbelievers and individuals whom we might consider as terrible sinners, receives a great many life-sustaining and wonderful gifts. People often consider these things as rights and that they deserve to enjoy them or that they are the payment for hard work. Christians recognize them as gifts from God. These *blessings* flow from God's grace and are undeserved gifts that come to us without any merit in us. On the other hand, by his grace, God also shows us *mercy*, and as a result, we escape punishment for our sins. In the greatest and astounding contradictions of all times, we receive what we are not worthy of—blessings—but don't receive what we deserve, punishment.

How then do we live as believers knowing that we are blessed and shown mercy? There are many Bible passages that speak to that issue in both the Old and the New Testaments. We are not perfect, but we have been liberated from sin's power; therefore, "Live as people who are free, not using your freedom as a cover-up for evil, but living as servants of God. Honor everyone. Love the brotherhood. Fear God. Honor the emperor" (1 Peter 2:16–17). Peter is saying that we must serve God, respect and love our neighbor, and obey the government. We are also to fear God. Does this mean that we're to live in constant and overwhelming dread of our God? I don't believe so. In the *Small Catechism*, a handbook written to facilitate teaching the basic doctrines of Christianity, Martin Luther begins his explanation of each of the Ten Commandments with "We should fear and love God." In this usage, fear means to stand in awe of the Lord, treat him with the utmost respect, and hold him in the highest reverence.

The word fear is also used with its more common meaning of terror in many passages. Interestingly, that sense is often associated with the appearance of angels with messages for humans. That was the case for a man named Cornelius when an angel appeared to him with a message to bring the apostle Peter to the city of Joppa from the city of Caesarea. "About the ninth hour of the day, he saw clearly in a vision an angel of God come in and say to him, 'Cornelius.' And he stared at him in terror and said, 'What is it, Lord?'" (Acts 10:3–4). A more familiar example is the announcement of the birth of Jesus to the shepherds, "And an angel of the Lord appeared to them, and the glory of the Lord shone around them and they were filled with great fear. And the angel said to them, 'Fear not, for behold, I bring you good news of great joy that will be for all the people'" (Luke 2:9–10). Usually, the appearance of an angel or angels is so overwhelmingly terrifying that the first thing said by the heavenly messenger is, "Fear not!" Yet we do not have to quake and tremble uncontrollably before our God because Jesus has won for us a new relationship with and access to the Father. Only through him is this possible.

A few verses later, as the angel finished the miraculous announce-ment of the birth of Jesus, another interesting term appears. "And suddenly there was with the angel a multitude of the *heavenly host* praising God and saying, 'Glory to God in the highest, and on earth peace among those with whom he is pleased!'"(Luke 2:13–14). In this day of television, it sounds like a good title for a series. An image of a program with an angel narrating the stories and solving human problems may spring to mind. We might also think of a talk show on which the star is a beautiful young actress, the heavenly host, who interviews and engages celebrities in friendly banter. You may also think of the hospitality to guests for which Middle Eastern cultures are so often mentioned in the Old Testament. However, that is not how it is used here. It means many angels or heavenly beings. God is often called the LORD of Hosts in reference to his command of the angels and all creation. In many passages, heavenly host refers to an army of heavenly beings ready to do God's will. In other passages in the Old Testament, the term seems to include created celestial bod-ies. Worship of all types of the heavenly host was clearly forbidden by God. "And beware lest you raise your eyes to heaven, and when you see the sun and the moon and the stars, all the host of heaven, you may be drawn away and bow down to them and serve them, things that the LORD your God has allotted to all the people under the whole heaven" (Deuteronomy 4:19).

Therefore, as Christians with all this good news of the gospel, shouldn't we always be on top of the world going through life glad at heart and whistling a catchy tune like the old one by a man named Bobby McFerrin, "Don't Worry, Be Happy!"? Don't we receive God's multiple blessings? Don't we have his certain assurance that our sins are forgiven? Don't we have his promise of the sure hope of eternal life? What more can we ask? What more do we want? What more do we need? Why aren't we perpetually happy? Could it be that our faith is not good enough or strong enough? These are all questions that make us uncomfortable. When all is going well, a baby is born, or we get a better job, we feel blessed, and we are happy. During King Solomon's time, things were going very right for the Hebrews: "Judah and Israel were as many as the sand by the sea. They ate and drank and were happy" (1 Kings 4:20). This implies a state of well-being, even merriment. In good times, it is easy for us to be glad and celebrate.

Nowhere in the Bible does God promise Christians a rose garden or a life without problems or pain. In fact, in the first book of the Bible, God puts us on notice that there will be difficulties when he said to Eve, "In pain you shall bring forth children," (Genesis 3:16) and to Adam, "By the sweat of your face you shall eat bread" (Genesis 3:19). We are human. Our state of mind and our situation do change, sometimes with overwhelming rapidity and crushing severity. We become clinically depressed, we are diagnosed with a disease, or someone close to us dies. We don't feel so happy when one or more of such things happen to us. We might feel resentful or even angry with God. I believe that this is where true *joy* rather than *happiness* comes in. The prophet Habakkuk who apparently worked just before Judah was destroyed by the Babylonians provides an instructive example. In his short book, he raises a series of complaints with the LORD and asks how long it will be until the wicked are punished, and he describes the devastation of his nation that is to come. In spite of that, he gave us a wonderful statement of his faith saying, "Yet I will rejoice in the LORD; I will take joy in the God of my salvation. God the Lord is my strength;" (Habakkuk 3:18–19). He was not happy or merry but joyful.

Different versions of the Bible render passages pertaining to the concept of good feelings differently so that it is difficult to be specific. One version might use the words *happy* or happiness, another *glad* or *gladness*, and a third joy or *joyful*. However, I believe that there is a subtle but important often misunderstood difference between the feelings of merriment, gladness, or happiness and true joy. For the most part, our happiness depends on our circumstances and our emotions. The song "He Will Make Me Glad" is a peppy tune designed to lift our spirits and make us feel better. However, when my wife was diagnosed with cancer, I was neither glad nor happy before or after I sang it. When bad things begin to pile up and difficult times arrive, we are not merry or happy; but because of God's sure promises, we can still have joy in our hearts. There is a startling passage in Hebrews that advises, "Let us run with endurance the race that is set before us, looking to Jesus, the founder and perfecter of our faith, who for the joy that was set before him endured the cross, despising the shame, and is seated at the right hand of the throne of God" (Hebrews 12:1–2). Certainly, Jesus did not gleefully dance toward the cross with merriment any more than you or I would. He was not happy to be tortured or glad for the humiliation, yet he faced it with joy because he trusted the Father. Such joy depends not on us and how we feel, but rather that we believe God's sure promises. We are not always happy, but joy rises above circumstance. "For the kingdom of God is not a matter of eating and drinking but of righteousness and peace and joy in the Holy Spirit" (Romans 14:17). Joy is an abiding gift that is not dependent on the changing events of our life or our fickle feelings about them. We are not saved only when we feel good or close to God.

Important Words Not in the Bible

Truly edifying words are words that reveal the character and the promises and the activity of God. They're cross-centered words. They're words rooted in and derived from Scripture, words that identify the active presence of God.

—C. J. Mahaney

There are some words that do not appear in the Bible but are used to refer to or express several of the most important and fundamental teachings of the Scriptures. They were not written by the authors of the Scriptures or at least not used by the translators of the various versions of the Bible. Yet, we encounter them during worship as we listen and sing or when we read or study. They occur in songs, hymns, and Christian literature. The following are examples.

Over my life, I have heard many times in sermons and often read that I have been *absolved* of my sins through the redeeming sacrifice of my Lord Jesus Christ and that I receive *absolution* for them when a minister during a divine service or someone else privately pronounces, "Your sins have been forgiven." Therefore, I was surprised to learn that neither of the two words is found in the Bible. To be absolved of something is to be set free or pardoned from a debt. Because our debt of sin is monumental, absolution is a gift of immense value and comfort. Absolution is God's gift of hearing that we have been forgiven or set free from our sins. That Jesus commanded this practice is documented by Saint Paul when he wrote, "Bearing with one another and, if one has a complaint against another, forgiving each other; as the Lord has forgiven you, so you also must forgive" (Colossians 3:13). It is important to read carefully and note that the Lord's forgiveness is a passed event—done once and for all. We have not only the right to forgive others but also the obligation to do so. I was surprised to read that absolution is "also sometimes considered a sacrament and thus a means of grace by Lutherans" (Lutheranism 101, p. 102). However, it is more commonly considered a *rite*. This is not the same as when we say, "I have a right to do what I want to do," or "We all have these rights under the constitution." In this sense, it is a formal religious practice or ceremony. A wedding is another example of a rite practice by Lutherans.

The important principle of our religion is that because of the work of Jesus, God sees us as blameless and withholds the punishment that we deserve for our sins. There is a remarkable passage that encapsulates that concept. "For our sake he [God] made him [Jesus] to be sin who knew no sin, so that in him we might become the righteousness of God" (2 Corinthians 5:21). The word *imputes* is used for that action. The term means to ascribe to or credit something to another thing or person. In another amazing and incomprehensible act, God accepts the most one-sided exchange in history, and there have been some big ones. How about the Dutch buying Manhattan Island for about $24.00 in beads or the Boston Red Sox trading Babe Ruth to the New York Yankees for about $100,000? Not even close! God not only imputes—in effect, trades Christ's righteousness to us for our unrighteousness—but also imputes our sins to Jesus. Here "turnabout is unfair play" and something that should be sobering to each of us. Christ died on a cross! We go free!

One afternoon, I was using the old fashion but still effective Yellow Pages to find the telephone number of a church that I wanted to contact. As I scanned the listing of churches, I noticed an entry for *Incarnation Church*. Now, that's an interesting and unusual name. The word is somewhat archaic and not commonly used. It stands for the very important concept—that of the embodiment of God in the person of the man Jesus. That God took on human form in the person of Jesus is called *incarnation*. If you think about this for even a moment, that God would come into human history for any reason let alone to provide a path by which we are declared righteous, it is mind-numbing. In a sermon a few days before one Christmas, the Pastor said, "Incarnation could be another name for Christmas." That statement amazed me and focused my thoughts on the fact that, yes, the baby Jesus whose birth we celebrate is the incarnation of our God. This is another concept that is impossible to fully grasp. How can God be a human and a human be God? The word is not used in the Bible, but it is clearly taught. The apostle Paul wrote, "He [Jesus] is the image of the invisible God, the firstborn of all creation" (Colossians 1:15). As the incarnation of the invisible God, Jesus came into the world to do what humans are unable to do—obey the requirements of the law.

If you attend a Sunday church service or a special midweek service in the weeks leading up to Easter, you will hear the pastor or lector read, in some form or other, the treatment that Jesus received from the Romans and Jews after his arrest. The torture, suffering, abandonment by God, and death of Jesus are referred to as his *passion*. This is not what we mean when we say that we are passionate about our job or my passion is saving whales. This was deep and searing agony, humiliation, and scorn inflicted by his captors. Jesus was abused unmercifully and ultimately put to death in a most painful way by being nailed to a wooden cross. A number of years ago, the movie *The Passion of the Christ* vividly depicted the brutality of crucifixion. Many viewers winced, and some were unable to watch. Graphic as the film was, the reality was more disturbing and difficult to take in. During his passion, Jesus was separated from the Father, and he bore the full weight of God's hatred of sin. What is incomprehensible is that he endured it "for you, for me, for everyone!"

The *Holy Trinity* is another of the great mysteries of Christianity that cannot be explained but must be accepted by faith. The concept refers to the truth that in the one God, there coexist three persons: the *Father*, the creator of the universe; the *Son*, the savior of sinners; and the *Holy Spirit* also called the *Holy Ghost*, the creator and sustainer of faith. The word trinity does not appear in the Bible, but references to the work of the three occur throughout, and the triune nature of

God is clearly taught. A wonderful example is Paul's blessing in 2 Corinthians 13:14, "The grace of the Lord Jesus Christ and the love of God and the fellowship of the Holy Spirit be with you all."

Words of Relationships:
The Son of Whom?

For to us a child is born, to us a son is given; and
the government shall be upon his shoulder, and
his name shall be called Wonderful Counselor.
Mighty God, Everlasting Father, Prince of Peace.

—Isaiah 9:6

What's in a name? Unfortunately, for some, in the time of casual
and confusing encounters, the answer may be "very little."
However, for many of us, our name, particularly our surname, ties
us to our family and our heritage. It connects us to our ancestors
and can be very significant if we are related to a rich, powerful, or
famous individual. We have previously used the names Savior and
Redeemer as they are used to refer to Jesus. There are many more,
in fact; Lutheranism 101 has a list of 101 names and terms for him
(p. 41).

Three of the names on that list refer to Jesus as the Son of someone. One name that is not included occurs in Matthew 1:1 where he
is inferred to be the *Son of Abraham*. Most commentators seem to
regard that reference as pertaining to David as the son of Abraham.
But as mentioned earlier, Abraham was considered the father of
the Hebrew nation to whom God gave the promise that one of his
descendants would be a blessing to all people (Genesis 22:17–18).
He is therefore rightfully considered an ancestor, a "father" of the

man, Jesus. The Jews of Jesus's time were extremely proud of their descent from Abraham and mistakenly believed salvation was guaranteed by that relationship alone. John the Baptist forcefully dispelled that false notion when he called the *Pharisees*, members of a religious and political party, snakes and said, "And do not presume to say to yourselves, 'We have Abraham as our father,' for I tell you, God is able from these stones to raise up children for Abraham" (Matthew 3:9).

The first verse of Matthew also names Jesus as the *Son of David*. Matthew and Mark also record that when Jesus entered Jerusalem before his arrest and crucifixion, he was called the Son of David by a large crowd of supporters. That title not only indicated that he was a descendent in the royal line of David but also had Messianic connotations. The term was well known to the Jews and might have contributed to or resulted from their expectation of a restored kingdom of earthly power. Messiah is used in both Old and New Testaments but only directly applied to Jesus after he came to fulfill the prophecies in New Testament time.

Jesus frequently used the expression *Son of Man* when speaking of himself. In fact, it was his favorite reference to himself possibly to emphasize his humanity. It is as if Jesus was saying, "I am the son of a woman; the son of Mary," to further illustrate his earthly connection. The title was not widely known as was Son of David and, in contrast to that title, seemed to have little if any connection to prophecy. Interestingly, the title occurs at least once in the Old Testament. In the book of Daniel 7:13–14, it says in part that in one of his visions, Daniel saw "one like a son of man," who "was given dominion and glory and a kingdom, that all peoples, nations, and languages should serve him," and "which shall not pass away." This is certainly not a reference to a human ruler or an earthly kingdom that does not endure forever. Jesus also used the term when he demonstrated authority well beyond that of a mortal as he did when some *Scribes*, experts in the Law of Moses and associates of the Pharisees, questioned his right to forgive the sins of a paralytic man. He said to them, "But that you may know that the Son of Man has authority on earth to forgive sins—he said to the paralytic—'I say to you, rise, pick up your bed and go home'" (Mark 2:10–11). The man did so immediately, demonstrating to the amazement of the observers Jesus's right and ability to forgive sins as well as to heal the body.

But most importantly, Jesus is called the *Son of God* in a number of noteworthy situations. Jesus is first given the title at his *annunciation* when the Archangel Gabriel announced to Mary his forthcoming birth. When Mary questioned how she, a virgin, could give birth, she was told, "And the angel answered her, 'The Holy Spirit will come upon you, and the power of the Most High will overshadow you; therefore the child to be born will be called holy—the Son of God'" (Luke 1:35). At his birth, the angels identified him to the shepherds as *Christ the Lord*. Years later, just before Jesus began his public ministry, he was baptized in the Jordan River by his cousin John the Baptist. There the Holy Spirit came upon him and said, "And behold, a voice from heaven said, 'This is my beloved *Son*, with whom I am well pleased'" (Matthew 3:17). One evening near the end of his ministry, Jesus took several of his disciples up on a mountain to pray. There, his appearance was changed, and two Old Testament prophets appeared with him. "And he was *transfigured* before them, and his face shone like the sun, and his clothes became white as light. And behold there appeared to them Moses and Elijah, talking with him" (Matthew 17:2–). There as you, I, or anyone would be, the disciples with Jesus were terrified. Peter, one of the disciples, offered to build shelters for them, but "He was still speaking when, behold, a bright cloud overshadowed them, and a voice from the cloud said, 'This is my beloved Son, with whom I am well pleased; listen to him'" (Matthew 17:5). In each of these instances, Jesus was called God's Son directly by God himself or by his angelic messengers. There is at least one more occurrence recorded by both Matthew and Luke. When Jesus died, there was a great earthquake, and the temple curtain was ripped in two. "And when the *centurion*, who stood facing him, saw that in this way he breathed his last, he said, 'Truly this man was the Son of God!'" (Mark 15:39). A centurion was a Roman commander of one hundred men. This is an amazing statement by a man who was not only a soldier but also a Gentile.

As I listened to a praise choir sing the song "We Will Glorify," during a worship service, I was struck by the words. The first verse states we will glorify, that is, praise the great I AM. I am who, or I am what? How do I understand that term? I was aware that God and Jesus in particular are given a number of different names in the Bible. In the Old Testament written in Hebrew, several different words for God were used that are most often translated as the English words Lord, sometimes spelled with all capital letters [LORD]. However, one name stands out in the Old Testament because God applied it to himself! When God called Moses to go to the Israelites and represent them before the Egyptian Pharaoh, Moses hesitated as most of us would if we were asked to confront a powerful ruler. He was not even sure that the Israelites would accept him as their leader, so he inquired of God about whom he should say sent him. "God said to Moses, 'I AM who I AM.' And he said, 'Say this to the people of Israel, I AM has sent me to you'" (Exodus 3:14). God further explains that he is the God of Abraham and the patriarchs and that Moses had authority sufficient to represent him. Remarkably, Jesus applies that same name to himself in the New Testament in a discussion with Jewish leaders who, as always, were attacking his ministry. When Jesus noted that Abraham was glad to see his day, the Jews became enraged. "So the Jews said to him, 'You are not yet fifty years old, and have you seen Abraham?' Jesus said to them, 'Truly, truly, I say to you, before Abraham was, I am'" (John 8:57–58). Thereby, with his own testimony, Jesus confirms his relationship with God.

There is one more relationship that is extremely vital for us. It is a relationship so astounding that it is indeed breathtaking. When we first understand, it is the most important "aha!" moment that we will ever have. The apostle John clearly states the wondrous truth. "See what kind of love the Father has given to us, that we should be called *children of God*; and so we are" (1 John 3:1). As believers in Jesus Christ, we become sons and daughters of God! That relationship is not established by us. It is not predicated on who our ancestors were, how we feel, what works we do or don't do, or how strong our faith might be. It is not about us. The sure promise is founded on God's grace and given through the redemptive work of his Son, Jesus, who welcomes us as brothers and sisters. Faithful Christians then are the spiritual children of Abraham as promised so long ago. Surprisingly, the lines of a TV commercial shown often in my home city aptly fit the situation: "It can't get any better than that now, can it?"

Words of Power!

The power behind words lies with the person.

—Renee Ahdieh

The New Testament records many words spoken by Jesus that have powerful implications. In fact, one could argue that all of his words are powerful. He spoke words of instruction, rebuke, correction, healing, comfort, and forgiveness to many people, many times in many places. There are examples that are simply astounding that long-time Christians read overthinking, *That's just Jesus speaking. I've heard it many times over the years*, and that nonbelievers or new Christians might say, "Can I really take the words seriously? I don't believe them." When we, Christians overlook them, we lessen the deep comfort of those words; and unbelievers who reject them never find comfort in them at all. My three choices demonstrate the power of Jesus over nature, temporal death, and sin.

The first demonstration is recorded in three of the four gospels: Matthew, Mark, and Luke. On this occasion, Jesus spent a long day teaching large crowds with parables. Mark tells us that on that evening, he and his disciples got into a boat and started to cross the Sea of Galilee. Jesus soon fell asleep in the stern of the boat, and as he slept, a violent storm threatened to swamp the boat. It must have been quite a storm because a number of the disciples were experienced sailors and fishermen yet they were afraid and called for Jesus. What happened next had to amaze everyone present and should amaze us as well. "And he awoke and rebuked the wind and said to the sea, '*Peace! Be still*' and the winds ceased, and there was a great calm" (Mark 4:39). A few simple words and the forces of nature obey. This is reminiscent of what God said when troubles abound in one of my favorite passages, "Be still, and know that I am God" (Psalm 46:10).

The following instances display Jesus's compassion and his power over temporal death. The first case is recorded only by Luke and occurred as Jesus was approaching the town of Nain. There he and his disciples met the funeral procession of the only son of a widowed mother. He told the woman not to cry, "And he said, '*Young man I say to you, arise.*' And the dead man sat up and began to speak, and Jesus gave him to his mother" (Luke 7:14b–15). A second event is recorded by Matthew, Mark, and Luke. Shortly following the calming of the storm, Jesus was approached by a man named Jairus. The man's twelve-year-old daughter was dying, and he begged Jesus to come and save her. Though there are slight differences in the accounts of the three gospels, the girl died before Jesus arrived at the man's home. People were weeping and mourning for her, and when Jesus said that she was not dead but only sleeping, they laughed at him. Jesus, her parents, and three disciples went into her room and proved them wrong. "But taking her by the hand he called, saying, '*Child, arise.*' And her spirit returned, and she got up at once." (Luke 8:54–55). An even more astonishing example took place in the small town of Bethany where close friends of Jesus—Mary, Martha, and Lazarus—lived. When Lazarus became ill, the word was sent to Jesus who seemingly inexplicably tarried for several days, and before he reached the village, Lazarus had died four days earlier. When he did get to Bethany, he wept for his friend and asked to be taken to his tomb. Jesus consoled Martha, prayed to the Father, and then, "When he had said these things, he cried out with a loud voice, '*Lazarus, come out.*' The man who had died came out, his hands and feet bound with linen strips and his face wrapped with a cloth" (John 11:43–44).

My final power words were uttered by Jesus on the cross at the time of his death. Jesus said a number of things as he suffered crucifixion. He promised paradise to a dying thief on a cross next to him, and he provided for his mother's care. But for us, sinful humans, the most powerful words are his confident statement at his death. "When Jesus had received the sour wine, he said, '*It is finished*,' and he bowed his head and gave up his spirit" (John 19:30). These words of a dying man might seem like a questionable choice. They were spoken by a man who was not only dying but also dying under humiliating and shameful conditions. In reality, they refer not merely to the end of his suffering and life, but to the end of his work of redemption. They are amazing words that signify a mission completed and are made more so when they were stamped as true by God the Father when he raised Jesus from the grave and accepted his sacrifice on Easter morning.

This is a remarkable set of words that supply comfort and joy. Peace! Be still. Jesus not only stilled the storm on the Sea of Galilee but also provides us peace and stills the storms of our lives. Our war with God is over. Although the commands "Young man, come out," "Child, arise," and "Lazarus, come out" returned people to life only temporarily they give us great comfort. The declaration "It is finished!" states that Christ has vanquished death and the devil and that our hope is sure. Someday, he will take our hand and command, "*Child, come out* to eternal life." Thanks be to God!

Words of Comfort

Comfort, comfort my people says your God.

—Isaiah 40:1

B y now, you should be convinced that there are all kinds of words from and related to the WORD. Some words are used in our worship of our Lord even though we often take them only as an all too familiar part of a divine service and overlook them. We speak, sing, or read them and pass on without realizing their importance. That is unfortunate and something that we really must guard against because when something becomes too familiar, we are in danger of undervaluing it. Some words may confuse us, while others bring the sure promises of God to us. Some seem common but are much more. Other words illuminate our relationship with our God. Some speak to his awesome power. A few are not found directly in the Word but signify some of its most important concepts. Perhaps we now can appreciate the meaning of individual words such as *justification* or *atonement* and better understand passages in which words are tied together. Whether individual words or passages, they are there to instruct and deliver eternal truths. Yes, and thank the Lord, there are words of comfort, lots of them. They are liberally sprinkled throughout the Word in its broadest sense. We read them in the Bible or meditations. They are heard in sermons, in Bible study classes, and from the lips of friends. We sing them in hymns and contemporary songs. Different believers find comfort in different words, and the same believer can find different words of comfort for different times or situations in life. You may have your favorites words or passages already tucked away to be leaned on when adversity strikes. Here are my favorite words that comfort and sustain me. I have mentioned or discussed each in previous sections but they are worthy of another look.

Grace

This is it—what everything else is based on. Grace is more than God's love. Our entire relationship with God is due to his grace through Jesus. "Through Him [Jesus] we have also obtained access by faith into this grace in which we stand, and we rejoice in hope of the glory of God" (Romans 5:2). Because of his grace alone, he shows his love, saves, comforts, sustains, and blesses us. Grace is God's love in action. Not only does he love us, but also he shows it through his kept promises.

Faith

Faith is more than belief. Believing is one thing; faith is another. A sobering reminder of that was written by the Apostle James, "You believe that God is one; you do well. Even the demons believe—and shudder!" (James 2:19). Faith is another of God's gifts through the Holy Spirit. It is a deep and complete reliance on God to protect and direct our lives. "Trust in the LORD with all your heart, and do not lean on your own understanding" (Proverbs 3:5). Without faith, we do not have a solid base for our lives. I believe in my favorite professional baseball team, but I do not have faith that they will win the World Series every year. I believe in our government, but I do not have faith that they will always do the right thing. I do have faith that God will always do what is right and just. We can count on him.

Emmanuel

Many times before Christmas, I have sung the hymn "O Come, O Come Emmanuel" (LSB 357) that uses that particularly wonderful name meaning *God with us*. The words of that hymn make it clear that the reference is to Jesus; however, the song "Jesus, Name Above All Names" is more explicit. The first verse names Jesus as Savior, Lord, Redeemer, Living Word, and Emmanuel. This name for God particularly for Jesus comes from the Old Testament passage Isaiah 7:14 in which the word is spelled *Immanuel*. That passage is quoted in the New Testament by Matthew, "Behold, the virgin will conceive and bear a son, and they shall call his name Immanuel (which means, God with us)" (Matthew 1:23). What could be a better and more comforting name for God than Emmanuel—God with us? In truth, not only is he with us, but also he is us. Jesus was also fully human. There are many names by which we call God and Jesus. Some reflect his glorious majesty, awesome power, or mystery. This name strikes me as most appropriate for our God who promises to be near to us and who takes a personal interest in our lives. Our God is not a far-off impersonal deity or some anomalous spirit that we feel internally. Rather, God is always near to us and seeks the best for us even if we do not realize or appreciate it. What could be better than faith in a God that is not only full of grace but also near to us? We can call on him, and he hears us.

Joy

Joy is perhaps my favorite word. Joy is more than happiness. Joy results from God's grace that provides the gift of faith by the Holy Spirit in a near and loving God. "Though you have not seen him, you love him. Though you do not now see him, you believe in him and rejoice with joy that is inexpressible and filled with glory, obtaining the outcome of your faith, the salvation of your souls" (1 Peter 1:8–9). Joy does not depend on how we feel or the circumstances we find ourselves in. It is founded on God's promises that we know to be certain. Once we understand that God's grace provides faith in Emmanuel, joy is inevitable.

Children of God

This is an amazing and humbling title. How can we be called God's children when we are so often petty and vindictive? It is because of God's son, our brother Jesus, that we are adopted into God's family, which is another miraculous gift through God's grace. "But to all who did receive him, who believed in his name, he gave the right to become children of God, who were born, not of blood nor of the will of the flesh nor of the will of man, but of God" (John 1:12-13). What more could we desire than to be by grace the faithful, joyful children of Emmanuel?

Words of Action

There is a huge difference between those who
follow Christ by words and those who do so by
action.

—Gift Gugu Mona

There are words in the Bible that suggest or even demand action. Jesus used such words frequently. He said, for example, "Follow me," "Sin no more," "Pick up your bed and walk," and even, "Get behind me, Satan," when he rebuked Peter. There are two such action words that I believe many have some problem distinguishing. Many churches have mission statements, and we often hear leaders or members speak about the *ministries* and *missions* of their church. Yet there sometimes appears to be some difficulty distinguishing the meanings of those two words. A church was a member of a Lutheran school association and supported the elementary school and high school generously. However, the support for the schools appeared in the mission section of their annual budget. The schools were not truly missions any more than would be an individual school in their building and administered directly by the congregation. The association and the schools are best-considered parts of the congregation's ministry. The words ministry and mission, though somewhat overlapping in use, are distinctive as can be distinguished in the work of Jesus. Both are action words.

The Father gave Jesus, what appears to us, to be a most distasteful mission. In essence, it was to suffer and die! He was sent to fulfill the sayings of the prophets and the Scriptures concerning the Messiah—to satisfy the Law, which sinners could not accomplish, and to suffer crucifixion as payment for the sins of the whole world. The Father sent him, and Jesus never wavered in his pursuit of that mission. He went steadfastly on to Jerusalem and to the cross on that Good Friday in spite of the opposition of the authorities and the apathy of most contemporary Jews. He persisted and completed that mission even when his closest associates did not understand what was happening. He was sent with a purpose and accomplished his mission the critical significance of which we now recognize.

Ministry means to teach, train, and equip someone or a group to carry on the work and further the mission. Jesus accomplished his mission, and through his ministry, he prepared his followers to spread the gospel. During his life on earth, Jesus attracted many followers or *disciples*. Of these, he selected twelve men to be his closest associates whom he trained and equipped to carry out his ministry and spread the gospel message. A *disciple* is "someone who receives instruction from or follows a teacher." "In these days he went out to the mountain to pray, and all night he continued in prayer to God. And when day came, he called his disciples and chose from them twelve, who he named *apostles*" (Luke 6:12–13). The following verses, 14 through 16, name the twelve men he so designated including Judas, who betrayed him to the authorities in the last days of his life and was later replaced by a man named Matthias. Furthermore, Jesus bestowed special gifts on those twelve men. "And he appointed twelve [whom he also named apostles] so that they might be with him and he might send them out to preach and have authority to cast out demons" (Mark 3:14–15). An *apostle* then is "a special messenger" whom Jesus commissioned to continue his ministry and to whom he gave special abilities and powers. Several other leaders of the early church are also referred to as apostles even though they were not among the original twelve disciples. These additional men were at the forefront of preaching the gospel beyond the borders of Palestine and throughout the Roman Empire. The great missionary Paul, who had been a staunch enemy of the Christians, received his appointment as an apostle through a vision he received on the way to the city of Damascus. In another example, in Lystra, a city in what is now the country of Turkey, Paul healed a disabled man. The amazed people were about to worship them as gods, "But when the apostles Barnabas and Paul heard of it, they tore their garments and rushed out into the crowd, crying out, 'Men, why are you doing these things? We also are men'" (Acts 14:14–15). It is again important to note that Jesus chose these men to carry on his work and spread the gospel. They did not choose him.

The title *evangelist* also has been applied to Matthew, Mark, Luke, and John, the writers of the four gospels. In a general sense, an evangelist is "one who proclaims good tidings or good news." Paul wrote to a younger pastor, Timothy, "As for you, always be sober-minded, endure suffering, do the work of an evangelist, fulfill your ministry" (2 Timothy 4:5). So, what are we, Christians—disciples, evangelists, or apostles? The answers are, yes, maybe, and no. You, I, or anyone who follows Jesus is one of his disciples. We are evangelists when we bring his teachings to others as called workers or as laypersons through personal conversations with family and friends. We are not considered apostles. That is a title reserved for special men of the early church selected and commissioned by our Lord.

A mission then is a task or assignment that one is asked or commanded to complete. We know that soldiers are assigned missions all the time. Their mission might be mundane such as to complete the preparations for an important ceremony and parade. On the other hand, their mission might be much more significant and life-threatening when they receive an order to attack and capture an important enemy-held road intersection. For us, Christians, our most significant and important mission is recorded in Matthew 28:18–20 where Jesus says, "All authority in heaven and on earth has been given to me. Go therefore and make disciples of all nations, baptizing them in the name of the Father and of the Son and of the Holy Spirit, teaching them to observe all that I have commanded you. And behold, I am with you always to the end of the age." These words are known as the *Great Commission* with which Jesus commands his apostles and all his disciples to spread his teachings, that is, to evangelize the world in the name of the Triune God. This then is our mission. Our ministry is the training and equipping for and what we do to carry out that assignment. Pastors are trained in seminaries, teachers are trained in colleges, and lay members are equipped by worship and Bible study. Jesus clearly said not only "GO" but also "DO"—action words that many of us, his disciples, fail to carry out effectively or ignore completely.

Then there is the big one—*love*! Wow! That seems easy. Let's see; I love coffee, beef stroganoff, and pie. But wait; that's not real love. It is more that I like them and some of them I like a whole lot. How about people? Well, I love my spouse. I love my children. I love my parents and my best friend. That's more like it. That has to be a good thing. Let's see what the Bible has to say about love and the question of who should I love.

I am not going to get into the different kinds of love that are recognized. That is another topic. Rather, I want to look at whom we are to love. We hear the answers from several passages of Scripture. A passage from the Old Testament book of Deuteronomy provides a direct answer: "You shall love the LORD your God with all your heart and with all your soul and with all your might." (Deuteronomy 6:5). Okay, that's number one. It is an ancient command. I get that. This should be easy. The Lord has given me all things, yet I so often lose focus.

In the New Testament, Jesus answers this way, "A new commandment I give to you, that you love one another: just as I have loved you, you also are to love one another. By this all people will know that you are my disciples, if you have love for one another" (John 13:34–35). All right, I do love other Christians, especially the members of my congregation. We worship together, enjoy fellowship, and give and receive support in times of trouble. In addition, I know many people from attending activities at our parochial schools, serving on boards and committees, and going to fundraisers. Some of them are good friends. I guess in a way, I even love Christians whom I don't know and have never met because we share a common faith. So I am covered here; however, Ed is so overbearing in voter's meetings, and Margret can be so annoying when it comes to the organization of the church kitchen that they are difficult to love at times. I need Luther's advice to put the best construction on everything.

Another ancient command in Leviticus identifies an object of our love that takes us even farther from our comfort zone: "You shall love your neighbor as yourself" (Leviticus 19:18). Someone once asked Jesus to clarify who should be considered a neighbor. The Jews apparently considered fellow countrymen, who are other Jews, their neighbors. The answer Jesus gave in the parable of the Good Samaritan (Luke 10:25–37) does not define the term but indicates how to be a neighbor by showing consideration, compassion, and love to those we come in contact with every day. That includes the guy next door whose dog runs amuck on my front lawn as well as the aggressive and aggravating driver on the freeway.

Finally, Jesus really tosses out a challenge. He wants us to try to love those people who don't like us at all. Incredibly and incomprehensibly, he tells us, "You have heard that it was said, you shall love your neighbor and hate your enemy. But I say to you, Love your enemies and pray for those who persecute you" (Matthew 5:43–44). That means not only the annoying business competitor but also the dangerous gang member and the dedicated terrorist. I must admit that I am not very good at this; I hope that you are.

The Last Word

Come, Now is the Time to Worship.

—Brian Doerksen

During a Veterans Day ceremony at our local Lutheran High School, the speaker gave a thought-provoking message on military service, our national anthem, and patriotic words and actions and how they connect to our faith. One of his major points was that we too often do not listen to or appreciate the words of our national anthem. Those words are stirring because they relate the author's unease and dread as he awaits the dawn to determine if the fort has survived and if its flag is still flying and his relief when it becomes clearly visible. The words have a deeper meaning to the men and women who have stepped up to serve and defend our country with their actions. Their actions demonstrate love and devotion to our nation. Words and actions both matter! Similarly, we frequently do not listen carefully to or appreciate fully the words of the Word. Those words should have a deeper meaning than merely academic interest to us as Christians. Those words are stirring as well yet at the same time comforting. They prompt our actions. It is not that our actions have any saving merit; we know that is not the case. On the contrary, they reflect in our lives our love of and devotion to our Savior God who by grace first loved us. Words and actions both matter!

The last word has not been written or spoken yet. The beautiful song by Brian Doerksen warns, "One day every tongue will confess

You are God. One day every knee will bow." The apostle John states, "He who testifies to these things says, 'Surely I am coming soon.' Amen. Come Lord Jesus!" (Revelation 22:20). There will be more said when the Lord returns. In the meanwhile, John also wrote, "The grace of the Lord Jesus be with you all. Amen." (Revelation 22:21). These are indeed consoling words from the Word. God's promises in his Word are sure: "Forever, O LORD, your word is firmly fixed in the heavens" (Psalm 119:89). Meanwhile, "Your word is a lamp to my feet and a light to my path" (Psalm 119:105).

References

Kinnaman, Scot A., ed. *Lutheranism 101*. St. Louis, Missouri: Concordia Publishing House, 2010.

Lockyer, Herbert, Sr., ed. *Illustrated Dictionary of the Bible*. Nashville, Tennessee: Thomas Nelson Publishers, 1986.

Luecke, Geo. *Distinctive doctrines and customs of the Lutheran Church*. St. Louis, Missouri: Concordia Publishing House.

Mueller, Wayne D. Justification: How God Forgives (The People's Bible Teachings). Milwaukee, Wisconsin: Northwestern Publishing House, third printing, 2016.

The Commission on Worship of The Lutheran Church—Missouri Synod. Lutheran Service Book. St. Louis, Missouri: Concordia Publishing House, 2006.

The Holy Bible, English Standard Version (ESV). Crossway, 2001.

Wolfmueller, Bryan. *Has American Christianity Failed?* St. Louis, Missouri: Concordia Publishing House, 2016.

Appendix 1

The Ten Commandments

The LORD gave the Ten Commandments to Moses on Mount Sinai and wrote them on two stone tablets (Exodus 20:1-17; Deuteronomy 5:5–21). It is not known exactly what God wrote on each tablet, most commentators propose the following division of the text. The first tablet addresses man's relationship with God. The second tablet addresses man's relationship with other men. God did not intend for the commandments to be a set of laws by which salvation could be earned. These commandments show us our sin and our need for a savior. Although they were issued more than four thousand years ago, they are still relevant today as we strive to lead a Christian and God-pleasing life.

The First Tablet

> You shall have no other gods.
> You shall not misuse the name of the LORD your God.
> Remember the Sabbath by keeping it holy.

The summary of the first table is stated in the Old Testament as, "You shall love the LORD your God with all your heart and with all your soul and with all your might" (Deuteronomy 6:5).

The Second Table

Honor your father and your mother.
You shall not murder.
You shall not commit adultery.
You shall not steal.
You shall not give false witness against your neighbor.
You shall not covet your neighbor's house.
You shall not covet your neighbor's wife, or his manservant or maidservant, his ox or donkey, or anything that belongs to your neighbor.

The summary of the second table is stated in the Old Testament as, "You shall not take vengeance or bear a grudge against the sons of your own people, but you shall love your neighbor as yourself: I am the LORD" (Leviticus 19:18).

In the New Testament, Jesus answers a question about which is the greatest commandment saying, "You shall love the Lord your God with all your heart and with all your soul and with all your mind. This is the great and first commandment. And a second is like it: you shall love your neighbor as yourself. On these two commandments depend all the Law and the Prophets" (Matthew 22:37–40).

Appendix 2

Israel: Nation or Man?

The name Israel appears often in the Bible and is used in at least three different ways. Perhaps the most familiar is in reference to the Jewish or Hebrew nation, the chosen people of God. However, it is also the name of a specific Old Testament Patriarch and the name of one of the two nations formed when the Hebrew people divided after the death of Solomon.

God changed the name of the patriarch Jacob to Israel after he wrestled all night with a mysterious man. At the time, Jacob feared an impending confrontation with his estranged brother Esau. He was engaged in a spiritual struggle of prayer that manifested itself in a physical wrestling match with God. As dawn was breaking, an injured Jacob locked his arms around the man and would not let go until he received a blessing. The man then blessed Jacob and changed his name apparently to reinforce the lesson he was taught, that is, to hold fast to the LORD in all things (Genesis 32:22–32).

God had promised to make the descendants of the patriarchs into a great nation and to give them a land of their own. He renewed that promise to Jacob and sanctioned the name change. "God appeared to Jacob again, when he came from Paddan-aram and blessed him. And God said to him, "Your name is Jacob; no longer shall your name be called Jacob, but Israel shall be your name." So he called his name Israel. And God said to him, "I am God Almighty: be fruitful and multiply. A nation and a company of nations shall come from you, and kings shall come from your own body. The land that I gave to Abraham and Isaac I will give to you, and I will give the land to your offspring after you" (Genesis 35:9–12). This being the Old Testament nation of a united Israel.

After the death of the great King Solomon, his son Rehoboam became king. He followed bad advice, mishandled the transfer of power, which led most of the ten tribes living in the north to revolt; and the kingdom was divided. The split resulted in the formation of two separate kingdoms: Judah in the south and Israel in the north. "So Israel went to their tents. But Rehoboam reigned over the people of Israel who lived in the cities of Judah" (1 Kings 12:16–17). That situation remained until each was conquered, and the Hebrew nations ceased to exist as an independent entity.

Appendix 3

Angels

Angels are an order of spiritual beings created by God before the creation of the world. They are superior to man in intelligence and power but are not all-powerful and all-knowing. What angels look like is an unanswered question. The beautiful winged renderings of art have no basis in the Bible. Angels often appeared in human form; however, in some instances, they are described as very unhuman-like. In either case, angelic appearances usually caused terror in the humans involved, and the first words of the heavenly beings are "Fear not" or "Do not be afraid." By the way, we humans do not become angels when we die in spite of many movie portrayals.

There are several kinds of angels mentioned in the Bible:

Holy or unfallen angels

Angels are spiritual beings obedient to God, serve as his messengers, act as his agents for the destruction of evil, and protect man. They seem to compose a vast army or a heavenly host as attested to in both the Old and the New Testaments. Once when Syria invaded Israel and tried to capture the prophet Elisha, he prayed that his servant could see the LORD's protection around them, and the prayer was answered. "So the LORD opened the eyes of the young man, and he saw, and behold, the mountain was full of horses and chariots of fire..." (2 Kings 6:17). On the evening of Jesus's arrest, one of his disciples attacked the servant of the High Priest. In response, Jesus said, "Do you think that I cannot appeal to my Father, and he will at once send me more than twelve legions of angels?" (Matthew 26:53).

Archangels seem to be angels of the highest rank. Only two are named in the Bible: Michael, first mentioned in Daniel 10:13, and Gabriel, first mentioned in Daniel 8:16. Gabriel also had the honor of announcing the birth of both John the Baptist and Jesus as told in the first chapter of Luke.

Cherubim first appear in Genesis 3:24 when God placed a cherub at the Garden of Eden to guard the tree of life. In Exodus 25:10–22, God directs Moses to construct the ark of the covenant and to place two cherubim on its cover. In Chapter 10, Ezekiel describes the appearance and characteristics of the cherubim. They are not the sweet baby-faced little darlings so often seen in artistic renderings but rather awe-inspiring creatures.

Seraphim appear in the Bible only in Isaiah's vision of God when he was appointed to his ministry. They are beings with six wings seen flying around the throne of God and singing his praises. One also purified the lips of the prophet with hot coal (Isaiah 6:1–7).

The Angel of the Lord is a somewhat mysterious messenger from God mentioned many times in the Bible. He is usually considered the Lord himself while at other times seems to be one sent by God. He is a powerful being appearing in human form that allows him to interact with man.

Evil or fallen angels

Only two of these angels are named in the Bible. The chief and best known is *Satan*, which means adversary or enemy, although he is not so designated, who first appears in the third chapter of Genesis and is involved with the fall of humans into sin. He is first specifically called Satan in the book of Job although he is also called by a list of other names including Beelzebub and the more familiar, the devil, meaning accuser or slanderer. A second fallen angel may be Abaddon or Apollyon, who is called the angel of the bottomless pit in Revelation 9:11. There is one other reference in the King James Version of the Bible where he is called Lucifer in Isaiah 14:12.

About the Author

Dr. Ron Stieglitz grew up on a dairy farm in Wisconsin. He earned a BS from the University of Wisconsin-Milwaukee and advanced degrees in geology from the University of Illinois. He served a tour in Vietnam with the US Army, worked for the Ohio Geological Survey, and taught geology and environmental science courses for thirty years at the University of Wisconsin-Green Bay. He has held leadership roles in Lutheran congregations in several states. He loved playing baseball and softball until long after it was time to quit. He now patiently follows the Milwaukee Brewers. As professor emeritus, he lives in Green Bay, Wisconsin, with his wife Bev. They have four grown children, twelve grandchildren, and two great-grandchildren.

CPSIA information can be obtained
at www.ICGtesting.com
Printed in the USA
LVHW101515180422
716530LV00004B/193